THE LONELY ROAD

Novels by

William J. Schrader

KISS MY TEARS AWAY

THE HEALING ROAD

THE LONELY ROAD

William J. Schrader

iUniverse, Inc.
New York Lincoln Shanghai

THE LONELY ROAD

iUniverse books may be ordered through booksellers or by contacting:

iUniverse
2021 Pine Lake Road, Suite 100
Lincoln, NE 68512
www.iuniverse.com
1-800-Authors (1-800-288-4677)

Because of the dynamic nature of the Internet, any Web addresses or links contained in this book may have changed since publication and may no longer be valid.

The views expressed in this work are solely those of the author and do not necessarily reflect the views of the publisher, and the publisher hereby disclaims any responsibility for them.

ISBN: 978-0-595-45383-2 (pbk)
ISBN: 978-0-595-89697-4 (ebk)

Printed in the United States of America

To my beautiful and loving wife

Elizabeth

Contents

PROLOGUE

KISS MY TEARS AWAY—my first novel—is a love story, as is its sequel, THE HEALING ROAD. Readers liked the story and characters, but when I asked them questions regarding the philosophy that I'd slipped in between the love words, their answers were discouraging—most had become so involved with the story, they'd missed the message. I'd written the novels with a hope they would encourage the reader *think*, but I had failed. One reader, bless her heart, told me, 'I loved your book, understood and agree with your thoughts, but most of your readers are not ready for your message.'

My dear wife, Elizabeth, suggested I write a book about my philosophy—but with raised eyebrow—I responded, "Who wants to read philosophy written by an engineer? Even famous philosophers have a hard time getting read." She said, "Humor me—tell people how a boy, raised a Baptist, with a 'fire and brimstone' Baptist minister grandfather, evolved into a person with a philosophy so deep and beautiful as your own."

THE LONELY ROAD is the product of 'humoring' my wife and is an effort to reach other readers who might be 'ready for my message.' This book relates the life of a Christian man who chose to walk a *different* path, a path whereon he sought answers to questions too long hidden from him—the Truth. I was that man and I felt the Truth must weave its golden thread through all religions—however obscure and misunderstood that truth may be. I walked the path in search of that *golden thread*, and it became a very *lonely road*.

This book is written to that rare person who looks deep into the meaning of life and asks, *Why?*

1

I was frightened by a glaring light and then thrown down between two huge mounds to struggle in a terrifying cold; my hands could not comprehend those large objects that now towered over me and became mountains of frustration; all I could do was thrash and scream in protest at having been ripped from the security of my warm, dark home—a home from which I'd been too early torn.

Scores of years have dumped their episodes into my memory since then ... since that day when my three pounds of flesh arrived into this world two months early. It was April 14, 1929 and had been a beautiful Sunday afternoon, but now my survival swung on a pendulum of doubt. My mother had been having migraine headaches—a symptom of uremia that threatened to take her life and mine. The wastes had backed up in her body and kidney-shutdown seemed inevitable; then she suffered convulsions and was taken to the hospital in critical condition. In that ill-equipped little hospital in Ludington, Michigan she fought to bring me safely into this life.

My mother was too ill to care for me after we returned home; my sister Ruth had to quit school and care for us both. I was so tiny a shoebox could serve as a coffin if needed. Ruth solved the question of my life or death—she put me in a clothesbasket behind a potbellied stove and let me sleep for a couple months—it was before incubators had come to town.

I suspect my arrival was not planned, either before or at the time of my 'early descent,' because I was the eleventh child of my forty-four year old mother, and I came along six years after the birth of her tenth offspring. The first eight children were born in log cabins in the hills of Tennessee where my millwright father built lumber mills. My mother, Charity, was one of twelve children of the Reverend Joel and Mary

Jane Chitwood of Winfield, TN. Young Charity met my father and nursed him back to health after he'd had a life threatening mill accident in Sterns, KY. They married in 1905, he was twenty-three, she nineteen. You might say *I owe my life to a lumber mill accident … my life* and also the hundreds of progeny that followed as a result of that 'chance' union.

The family moved north to Michigan after they'd survived the Flu epidemic of the early 1920's (as the story goes) by receiving many doses of uncle Jarv's moonshine. In Ludington the last three of my generation were born. The first ten years of my life—the years of the *Great Depression*—were spent on the shore of Lake Michigan; those years that also comprised the *Great Depression*. My father worked for the Morton Salt Company, so my memories do not contain those of a constantly empty stomach; although we may have been counted among the poor, I didn't suffer the ill effects of starvation. We always had plenty of peanut butter, oatmeal and canned milk.

We lived in that old four-bedroom house on South Madison Street until I was ten years old. My memories of those years are only flashes … flashes of my mother's sweet voice singing hymns and telling me stories from the Bible. The Grand Old Opery on Saturday night radio was a ritual, and radio was a great source of entertainment for me … when the Lone Ranger was the tallest cowboy and fastest gun in the west, and his horse, Silver, was the fastest, biggest horse ever … It is sad how TV destroyed a world that had been created by my imagination, an imagination that when used at play, could turn a simple stick into a sword, a spear, or a Winchester repeating rifle. I lament for the children of today who have only high tech video games, cell phones and constant material satisfaction to saturate—but not inspire—their growing brains.

We moved thirty miles north to Manistee, Michigan in the spring of 1939. My parents rented an old four-bedroom house in a section of town that comprised a cross-section of affluent and 'struggling' families. We could still be counted with the 'struggling,' but my playmates knew no cultural segregation and I was lucky to be immersed in multiple levels of society. Religion was a case of going to Sunday school with friends—especially after our Baptist Church burned down. I was never exposed to a 'fervent' anything; even my Catholic friends were mild … they only complained about the nuns who beat them when they misbehaved.

I was exposed to piano lessons during my eleventh year but—having no piano—practicing on a paper keyboard was less than inspiring. I took violin lessons at the age of twelve when a neighbor gave me a violin. I learned 'that consistent practice' was *not* part of my nature. My mother might have inspired me to become another Heifetz—but I doubt it. She also might have made me do my homework and learn to do something with my mind besides daydream of flying airplanes.

My mother died of cancer in September of 1941, too sick to realize two of her sons, John and Lacey, had already been called into the Army and one son, Coney, into the Coast Guard. She hated war, having lost brothers in the first 'war to end all wars.' She would have suffered throughout the many years of WWII—and her pain would have peaked when Lacey was lost over the Mediterranean Sea in 1943. Her fourth son, Roger, was drafted that same year.

I moved in with my father and his new wife in late 1943, but within four months I moved out to live with my sister, Gloria. It allowed me to be 'near' school (only two miles instead of five and no bus service). My job at the Kroger grocery store allowed me to earn enough money to put myself through high school. In high school, although I played football and participated in extra curricular activities, I was painfully shy—especially around girls—and was voted "Most Bashful" in my class for four years running. I took flying lessons—when I could earn the money—but my high school grades probably never flew higher than the lowest twenty-five percent of the class.

I was too young to be called for WWII, but I enlisted in the Army Air Force in June of 1947 … to pursue my career as a fighter pilot.

2

A LITTLE MORE DETAIL

The early months of military life are never easy for a shy eighteen-year-old boy from the Midwest, especially when he comes from a small town on the west shore of Michigan like Manistee. My quiet demeanor, however, must have been misinterpreted as maturity, because I was immediately made a squad leader and soon after, Assistant Flight Chief, (A rarity for a Basic Trainee at Lackland Air Force Base, Texas, in the summer of 1947.)

The position was emotionally difficult for me however; I didn't fit-in with the Non-Commissioned Officers, because although I was in their leadership ranking, I was still a Basic Trainee. I didn't fit with the other trainees because I was an acting Non-Com. It was a lonely time for me, and as an escape I started keeping a journal … not of my day-to-day activities, but a record of my 'thoughts.' Those journals have traveled many thousands of miles in their lifetime, and although the hand writing, spelling and grammar now gives me cause to chuckle, I am amazed at some of the depth I had expressed. The frustration experienced and recorded by that young man sometimes makes me wonder at my sanity, but some of the thoughts exhibited give insight into my struggles in the distorted world of 'boys pretending to be men.'

I was not *always* alone; I had buddies with whom I did the things that buddies do, but I was never one to get drunk at every chance, nor did I chase after 'skirts'—not that I didn't want to—I just didn't have the know-how; my education in that realm was sorely lacking. It was another case where Schrader didn't really fit-in with the rest of the guys. The fact that I wanted to be an officer probably modified my

4

behavior to some degree. I believed, *officers are supposed to act better than the average G.I.*, and I wanted to be an outstanding officer.

I wanted to be an officer, but I also wanted to be a pilot, and when my eyesight excluded me from pilot training, I turned down an invitation to Officers Candidate School and at the end of my three-year enlistment, on 24 June 1950, I took an honorable discharge—the same day North Korean troops crossed over the thirty-eighth parallel into South Korea. I expected the Air Force to call me back at any time, and during that summer I feared the mailman's approach. I survived the mailman, and in September I became a student of Civil Engineering at Indiana Institute of Technology in Fort Wayne. (Okay, for you experts … it was called Indiana Technical College at that time.)

The war in Korea wasn't going well and there were threats of veterans being called back into service as Privates. The Indiana Air National Guard had a squadron locally, whose radio operators I'd train during their Summer Camp at Selfridge Air Force Base, Michigan. The local Commanding Officer remembered my performance at Selfridge and implemented his intense campaign to recruit me into his Squadron. The unit was less than half-strength and I 'knew' it would *never* be federalized—however, I was wearing the 'blue suit' again in eleven months, and in four more months I was ordered to report to California for shipment to the Far East.

◆　　◆　　◆

The 'foot-wanderings' of this old 'flyboy,' are not of sufficient interest to relate herein. I was no hero, won no medals and never fired a weapon at an enemy. No, this book is about the mind-wanderings of a man and how, after many years of thinking about it, he came to write a book of 'philosophy.'

Many years of my life came and went by the time I finished and published my first novel, and before the first was published I'd completed a draft of my second. My beautiful wife, Elizabeth, who had already suffered through the growing pains of becoming a 'writer's widow,' pressed me to write a book relating my thoughts and philosophy. "Why?" I'd asked, "Who would want to read a book about *my* thoughts?" She made me promise to 'think about it.'

I thought about it, and based on the comments from some readers of my first novel KISS MY TEARS AWAY, I realized that 'A love story with a message,' as I called it, wasn't reaching everyone; too many people only skim, they don't read. Too many readers of my novel saw only the love story and poetry—they'd missed the message—but the love story was meant to be only a *vehicle* to carry my philosophy, and I had failed to reach all those who ventured into those pages. I was trying to reach those who 'do not read books about God' but it didn't work. One reader told me, "Those who were not reached, are not ready." Perhaps the reader of *this* book will be ready.

◆   ◆   ◆

There is no love theme in THE LONELY ROAD, unless the reader can recognize the love in the heart of a man struggling to become an individual. Long ago I wrote this line, *If you would be an individual, let it not be a goal you seek, but because of a road you travel alone.* The road of the individual is indeed a lonely road, because there are few who will risk exclusion from the 'tribe' by thinking a doubt, or to lose the comfortable certainty of a life in the 'fold,' where all are absolutely certain of their 'glory' at the end of life. True, there are many who choose to be 'different' as an act of rebellion against the establishment, and there are many things in this world that inspire some to become rebellious, but this book is not concerned with those sojourners. In this book I am addressing that rare person who looks deep into the meaning of life and asks, *"Why?"*

It is certain there is an end to this life, but the question of what comes after has created cultures, shaped civilizations, caused magnificent temples and churches to be constructed … but at the cost of misery of those who toil under the whip of those who 'shape.' It is those same 'shapers' who have caused the dissolution of civilizations and cultures by waging countless holy-wars—all for the *glory* of God'—A God who neither asked for nor requires glory from Man.

It is the rare person who begins to doubt the farce of religions and dares to think for himself. He may seek a better answer to that question, *Why am I here?* … and behold, another traveler may turn his footsteps down the 'Lonely Road.'

A young woman in Muskegon, Michigan, with whom I shared a class in *Ethics,* expressed an interest to find 'answers.' The questions she asked of me were the questions to which I, too, had sought answers. I told her, "If you choose the path in search of those answers, then you must be willing to accept its companion 'loneliness,' for it is indeed a very *lonely road.*"

◆   ◆   ◆

I walked that lonely road, seeking the Truth, but also seeking someone with whom to share the thoughts and the quest. Sadly, the sharing was mostly with my journals; bits and pieces, scraps of thought that crossed my mind in those delicious moments of deep plunges into the realm of … *Why?* Where did my mind travel in those years? Where did it go to return with thoughts that never crossed my mind in my 'make-a-living world?'

I wrote a little poem in 1951 when I was but twenty-one years old and new in college. How did it go …

FOOTPRINTS

Often when I'm strollin'
  Or sitting here at ease,

> I let my thoughts go wand'rin'
> And do just as they please.
>
> Thoughts that go a-walkin'
> The corridors of time,
> And often leave me wond'rin,'
> 'Could such be thoughts of mine?'
>
> Now, some might call it dreaming,
> An' perhaps they could be right,
> But never was all dreaming
> Reserved for only night.
>
> Oft' the fruits of dreaming
> Are used in life, I find,
> And thoughts that go a-wand'rin'
> Leave FOOTPRINTS 'cross my mind.

The poem inspired me to set aside those *wand'rin'* thoughts in my journals and labeled them *Footprints*. Most of those ramblings were written down in a hurry—before the moment flew. To read some of those thoughts now I must ask, *Did I really understand those truths back then? But I was so young …*

◆　　◆　　◆

I have long pondered over the problem of organizing this book, and wondered how best to present my thought-growth. I decided to lay it out in chronological order, in hope it might show the progress of the slow and frustrating climb to my present position on the ladder of enlightenment. The 'top rung is not yet in sight, but neither is the muddy ground on which it rests. I would ask the reader to look on this book as an exchange of *ideas*. True, you cannot share *your* thoughts with me—that is my loss—but I ask that you read the ideas—chaff and grain together—then take and sift them; keep what is worth keeping, and with a breath of kindness, blow the rest away. (If I may paraphrase Craik.)

3

COLLEGE DAYS

I'd emerged from a small town, ignorant of the world and the infinite universe of ideas and things to be learned. I'd grown, step by tiny step as I wandered the closed community of military life, but had learned very little of the world outside that virtual walled-stockade. To this day, when asked about my military life, I can only answer … "It was very interesting and I don't regret it … but ooh, how I wasted those years; all the things I *could* have experienced—could have learned—were never realized because of my own lazy ignorance." I may have been ignorant … but ignorance can be fixed …

In September of 1950 I first set foot on the campus of Indiana Tech. in Ft. Wayne and found the challenge of a new world. The student body was one hundred percent male, so for a man who'd experienced limited success with girls, an all-male campus might have its advantage—no cute coeds to distract me from my studies. On the other hand, any campus—like the military—tends to be a limited community; and I needed exposure to *life*. I participated in non-college activities in local churches, YWCA organizations and part time work. I met local residents and made friends with non-students who had migrated to Ft. Wayne from out-state communities. I became exposed to a diversity of interesting people—and people with a diversity of interests—and I started to stumble out of my cave of 'small town tunnel-vision.'

Tunnel vision is not restricted to small towns but, my life had not been what one would call, 'enlightened.' I was the youngest of eleven children, but by the time I was old enough to glean worldly knowledge from my brothers and sisters, most of them had gone off to raise families or fight a war. I did have one person in high school who took me under his learned wing ... I recall when ...

◆   ◆   ◆

Mr. Krause, the English Literature teacher, walked up and down the aisles between desks and handed back the short stories students had written prior to Christmas vacation. He talked to the students as he passed out papers and said, "There were many good stories written for this assignment and I had a hard time picking the winner. Remember I told you before Christmas, the best short story would be sent to the short story contest at SIXTEEN magazine. His hands were now empty of papers, but so were mine; my story had been turned in late—but even an "F" paper would be returned. Did this mean I was going to flunk the class? I needed this credit to graduate and I needed my high school diploma to get into Air Force pilot training. Where was *my* paper??

Mr. Krause returned to the front of the room, picked papers off his desk, turned to the class and said, "Here is a short story I wish *I* could have written, and it is the winning paper. I'd like to read it to you ... He read ...

"The air was cool and crisp, and as I walked along, the leaves brushed aside with a music that helps to make up the beauty of autumn." He paused, shook his head slowly and said, "Gee, I wish I could have written that line." The reading continued until at long last he finished and a student asked, "Who wrote it?" Mr Krause said, "This story was written by Bill Schrader." Thirty astonished students turned and looked at *me;* the students were astounded because Bill Schrader—probably the most least-likely student in class—had written the best short story.

My face must have been beet red as it received all the eyes turned on it in disbelief ... all save those of the girl who sat directly in front of me; her smile and wink showed she harbored no disbelief or surprise, her eyes told me, 'I've known all along you were hiding your light under a bushel, Mr. Bill Schrader.

Mr. Krause became my friend. He had a warm smile and a quiet way about him that made one want to do well in his class just because he was interested in you as a person. He took an interest in me and encouraged me to become a writer. No one had ever shown an interest in my abilities, or told me I could do *anything* well. I was always somebody's 'kid brother.' I attained individuality only in my daydreams—and the dreams of piloting a P-38 in the Army Air Force overshadowed any thoughts of my studying to become a writer.

Mr. Krause did his best to convince me to go to college and study journalism, but being a pilot was the only thing I'd ever wanted to do—and too—I was putting myself through high school and had neither the money, the grades nor the self-confidence to attempt a conquest of college. Eleven days after high school graduation I was sworn into the U.S.A.A.F.

Air Force life helped me to develop self-confidence and taught me that, in spite of low grades in high school, I wasn't such a dummy after all—lazy and ill-focused perhaps—but not stupid. During my travels, Mr. Krause corresponded with me, and when I would return home on leave, he insisted on our spending time together—when he would continue his efforts to inspire me to write. Mr. Krause died of a heart attack several years later, when I was in the Far East.

◆   ◆   ◆

It was in my first months of college that I recorded my slow growth of awareness. I was becoming aware of a universe that had vibrated around me for twenty-one years, but I'd hardly perceived.

Flipping through the pages of my journals of those early college days, I can see they reflect a seeking of wisdom … for instance …

30 October 1950

"Dear Lord, please help me to be unselfish in all things I do. Help me to wash fear and hate from my heart and my thinking. Help me to hide my sorrow and my heartaches so that I might be the only one to suffer from them. Help me to smile and to love and be friendly to all those people with whom I come in contact. Help me to help them. Give me an understanding heart that I might understand people, and then give me wisdom that I might use that understanding wisely. Help me to give of myself. What I have—let me share with others; what I have to give, let me give to others. Help me to be thoughtful of others."

I cannot but wonder what inspired me to write some of the things I find in those journals.

Three days later I wrote:

2 November 1950

"I was elected Treasurer of the Mixer Council tonight. (It was an organization at the YWCA that sponsored dances and functions for single adults.) Well, at least I've made a little headway in my effort to belong.

"Lester (my roommate) asked me why I do things like that; why do I work on the Council and do all those things for no pay. I couldn't think of any answer other than, 'I enjoy doing things for others for nothing.' I think that's the reason, because as long as I can remember, I've liked to do things for people—so long as I didn't think they were taking advantage of me. It isn't that I'm good or anything; I've always liked to make people happy, even thought for awhile in years gone by I got tired of it when all my efforts were turned down and crammed down my throat. It is different here. Here it gives me a feeling of belonging—a feeling of being wanted. I want to belong. I have no home; perhaps I can find a home with people. If somewhere I am wanted, then there I can call home. Perhaps I can make the world my home. Perhaps, for awhile, I can forget how I long for the love of a woman—that I can love equally as well.

"Please, dear Lord, don't let me become too pleased with myself. Don't let me become boastful. Help me to become more considerate of others, *all* others. Please, please don't let me feel sorry for myself. Let me put myself aside and give to all others.

"If I am wrong, dear Lord—and I don't think I am, because I have asked your help—then please show me the right way.

"Perhaps I can someday look back on this journal as a record of the evolution of W. J. Schrader—through God. Show me the way. Amen." (I can't help but reflect on those words, written over fifty-six years ago, that foretold my efforts of today.)

You read the lines above and might be led to believe I was raised in a religious home—I was not—a prayer of grace may have been uttered on occasion, perhaps before a Thanksgiving dinner. My mother taught me to be a good boy, but I don't recall having religion pushed at me … I wasn't even baptized … (Baptists didn't baptize babies and my mother was a Baptist.) I attended Baptist Sunday school until the only Baptist church in town burned down; after that, friends invited me to their Congregational church and in high school I considered myself a Methodist. In all probability, my church attending was more to be with friends than it was inspired by ministers.

In college I became active in the Methodist Church; I sang in the choir, attended church *and* Sunday school, plus a Sunday night group for the twenty and thirty age group. It was a good place to meet girls—pretty much the *only* place, outside of bars—and bars for a man on a G.I. Bill income was out of the question—seventy-five dollars a month didn't go far even in those days. This was also a time when I started reading the Bible's New Testament—a chapter a night before bed.

Reading the Bible by myself had advantages over sermons and Sunday school; I could pause and reflect—I could ponder and *question*. I didn't understand all I read, but the wise and learned told me, *God didn't intend for us to understand everything. We can never hope to comprehend the mystery of God's universe ...*

My journal tells me I was 'sworn-in' to the Indiana Air National Guard on 13 November 1950. My journal tells me also, I was not oblivious to women during this period. Prior to this, I'd known only teenage girls—with all the games girls play on boys. In the church group I met a woman that opened my eyes to the reality, 'all females are not girls—some are women.' Memories now recall the pain, joy, chills, warmth and the million emotions that assailed my life in those times.

The following excerpt from my journal of 15 November 1950 brings only warmth, and I wonder what ever happened to that woman, because I would like to say, "Thank you."

"... I've found a girl that has changed my ideas about love, life and marriage. This girl, of whom I speak, has awakened me to what love really is; what happiness life can hold with only simple things. She has made my life worth living and I've found contentment in just talking with her. She has brought into light the emotion I thought to be love and exposed it as an imposter. I thought what I felt with some others was love, when it was only the excitement aroused by necking. Those affairs were like the coals of a fire that glow when fanned, but die when the wind is gone. Can a marriage be built on a foundation of half-burnt coals? What then when the coals are ashes? If there were only the coals in the beginning, then nothing but ashes can remain, and two lives can be wasted. But to build a marriage on friendship, friendship that grows and mellows without the presence of the blinding cloak of passion and idolization, is to build your house upon a rock.

"Then what is this emotion I feel for Marcella? If it is love, then love is a stranger, for never before has such light been brought into my life by one person. A man asked me last night, 'Is she good looking?' I couldn't answer; to tell the truth I've never taken time to weigh her beauty against the standards known to others. To me, she is beautiful, but to me, her beauty comes from within. It can't be only skin deep if it comes from within. She likes to do things for other people. When it comes to tact, she is strictly 'on the ball.' I've never known a girl that can handle herself so well with people in general, as a hostess, as a leader and especially with me.

"I've been careful not to say I love her, for too many times in these journals have I written of my love for some girl—so many times that it leaves the word empty and meaningless. What I feel for this girl is not empty, it is full and wholesome and good—its meaning is life itself. No, instead, I shall merely state a fact; I have found new meaning in life through simply knowing the friendship of one particular girl.

"This will probably be all I'll ever write about her, because I doubt if a marriage or even a romance will be constructed upon our friendship. I will call this feeling—or change—simply, 'Marcella.'

"Marcella, whom I met at church.

"Marcella, who is at least four years my senior.

"Marcella, who has brought to me more happiness in three short months than I experienced in all the past twenty-one years. And she has done it without a word, without a sign, without a touch. She has done it by simply being herself.

"The winds of life are strong and bitter, but can be sweetened by the love of a woman."

In the words I wrote six days after the lines above, it is evident I was already wondering why I am here. Prophetic words, because fifty years later I wrote an answer to the questions in my novel KISS MY TEARS AWAY; but on 21 November 1950 I wrote …

"I wonder, are we brought into this world for one reason? Have we a mission to do and then pass on? Are we all but pieces of a large pattern? If so, will I know when my job is done? I hope I never know; because when I am working for something I am happy. Is Marcella a piece of the pattern of my life? Will Marcella help me to accomplish my mission? Someday I'll know all these things—someday in Heaven."

Several months passed and my friendship with Marcella mellowed; we were comfortable with one another—if not lovers. It is obvious in my journal that I was emotionally tied to her, but it is also obvious I never knew her true feelings toward me. Early in 1951 I learned that she was leaving Ft. Wayne to go to school in Arizona. The impact of her impending departure is evident in the poetry that suddenly sprang forth in my journal on 28 January 1951. Though I never considered myself to be a poet, the occasional desire to write verse cannot be separated from my desire to write philosophy—therefore, please bear with me …

"On Marcella's Leaving

My love did walk on cat feet
    Across the sands of time,
And 'long the way my heart did dance
    And sing each merry rhyme.

But that was long, so long ago
    A week were it a day,
Now one from out—I know not where
    Has born my love away.

My love no longer walks the sands
    That was our joy of meeting,
And now my heart—though young and brave
    Has taken to merely beating."

I must have been on a 'roll,' because on the next page I continued
with …

"Consolation

I should not be a weeping,
I should not cry in pain,
For even though I loved and lost,
I cannot say in vain.

It's all a part of living,
The part that's most worthwhile,
And even though I sorrow now,
It's only for a while.

So, come heart do your breaking,
For I can bear your pain,
And with the morrow's dawning go—
In search of love again."

Marcella left Ft. Wayne on 25 February 1951 and another poem
was penned:

"Marcella Left This Noon

The sun will rise tomorrow morn'
And after that the moon,

But life for me will be forlorn
Marcella left this noon.

Oh spring will come again this year,
And after that is June
But spring for me can ne'er be near,
Marcella left this noon.

Oh life for me was one sweet song
I treasured every day,
But now my days are cold and long,
Marcella's gone away.

Perhaps someday we'll meet again,
Just when I cannot say,
(.........)
Marcella went away."

I never finished the poem—a line was always missing—but it is perhaps fitting that I never found the right words for that line because, like Marcella, she was missing from the rest of my life and only the memory remains. If Marcella ever reads this book, she will recognize herself, and what she was in the life of a boy learning to be a man. Thank you, Marcella. (The next and last time I saw Marcella she was in uniform—a Marine uniform.)

◆   ◆   ◆

Time had a way of moving quickly when I bounced from class to class, test to test and activity to activity. Still I had time to reflect, and it was sometime in March when I scribbled …

FOOTPRINTS

"Life and love are as a single grain of sand in an hour-glass; of such great importance only as it passes from the upper to the lower glass, and though insignificant there in the lower glass, the hour is not complete without it—and yet, time would not stop if one grain of sand failed to pass—and without the hour-glass there is still time."

There is no indication in my journal pages as to what precipitated that bit of young wisdom, but I can't deny it still sounds good. Many of the things I wrote then were scribbled on scraps of paper, backs of envelopes, paper napkins and all sorts of media that witnessed my thoughts—written in a flurry without prior contemplation or later modification. The pen may have been in my hand, but the words hardly touched my mind as they flowed down through my fingers and on to the paper without pause. When reading what I have written, I hesitate to say that *I* wrote a truth, but if it was not *my* mind that uttered these thoughts, then whose?

The 8 April 1951 entry into my journal casually mentions, "We are being activated on November 1, 1951 ..." Our Air National Guard squadron was being federalized to participate in the Korean War. Six days later, on 14 April 1951, I turned twenty-two.

In September I made a trip 'home' to Michigan. I must have carried my journal along, because I wrote of sadness ...

"FOOTPRINTS: 2 September 1951 Manistee, Michigan.

"Tonight is Saturday and I sat in a tavern drinking beer and watching people; and I wondered what is so bad about the other six days of the week that makes so many people try to forget them on Saturday night.

"I saw married people—with both persons of the couple—wandering separately from table to table making asses of themselves. Can so many people make so many mistakes in marriage? Is life so dull and empty that only alcohol can sustain it? Oh Lord, surely there must be more in life than 'one too many beers on Saturday night.'

"I wondered, what do these people do during the week—what passes through the minds of the wives as they tolerate their drunken husbands—what weakness is there in a man or marriage that drives him to retreat to a drunken stupor whenever the occasion arises. Have they done so poorly a job of choosing a mate that they must drown out the pain with liquor? Why do people marry if they can't bear each other's company?

"I have been looking for a girl that can keep me interested without having to neck passionately with me. If not, then what is there after the wedding—can you keep the fires of passion burning constantly for sixty years? No—you must go out and get drunk on Saturday night.

"There was only one kind of person out there tonight—the lonely. Some were married, some were single, some were with dates, some were alone—but all were lonely.

"I'll get married someday, yes, but I won't get drunk on Saturday night."

◆   ◆   ◆

Autumn rushed toward 1 November, and the sounds of war grew louder in our ears. The men and boys of my squadron stared toward the activation date with mixed emotions—mingled with the emotions of their wives, girlfriends and loved ones who looked in fear at that same day, and all the days to follow. I scribbled a kind of a poem in the waning days of October ...

"To Arms!

My life of sun is over now
What follows is the rain,
A journey into darkness now
Where rest may come again.

Too often lives of sunshine end
When sounds of battle call,
And on the shoulders of our youth
The wars of old men fall.

This life is good, but life is short
So we should live it well,
What better asked, to leave it all
To die for freedom's bell.

I leave you life to fight a war,
Oh many were your charms,
How sad to hear your mating call,
'To Arms, To Arms, To Arms."

A short reflection on going off to war was written in October …

"… Life will not cease, even for me. My 'Good Mornings' may not be as pleasant as they once were, and my patience may grow a little shorter, but after awhile, the sun will shine as brightly as before and the future holds promise of new love—even thought her name might be 'Death;' and even after this, the sun will shine as brightly, and the lark will sing as sweetly, and green grass will grow … and I will little know."

On 1 November 1951 I answered the 'Call to arms,' and put on the blue uniform again. The idea of spending a lonely two years back in the Air Force, with no girlfriend waiting for my return, had a depressing effect on my days and nights. The confusion and frustration that occurred during the first month and a half of activation are too aggravating to relate here, but the one saving grace was Joan. We met and 'fell in love' during my first days of activation, and what once promised to be an easy departure for me, became extremely painful for both of us.

◆   ◆   ◆

Ink flowed freely through my pen in those days, but sadly, mostly in the form of love letters that have long since been lost and forgotten. The writing of those letters, however, served to keep me from the self-pity and loneliness that plagued my previous military days. My journals traveled thousands of miles, but the few pages in them that witnessed my thoughts, recorded only pitiful ramblings and mumblings, grumbled incoherently in my confusion of trying to phantom the workings of the female mind.

On 30 March of 1952 while on maneuvers in Brady, TX there was a glimmer of light in my confusion when I wrote:

"There is a word called 'conformity.' The word in itself is nothing; the effect it can have on people can be disastrous. What has happened to the American people to make them lose their individuality? Why have people become so afraid of stepping out of line, of being just a little different than others on the block? Everything they do and work for is merely a relative thing ... They work to have a little more than the man next door, but with no other reason than to out-do him or make themselves look better than *him*. They have no desire to work to look better than *themselves* ... "

I wrote on to include Joan's church, with whom I had obviously come to disagree ...

"There is a man in my squadron from Joan's church in Ft. Wayne; we went into town to his church early today and then had breakfast and went to a Methodist Church. Later he told me 'I felt very uneasy going to your church today.' I asked him why. He said, 'Because I am a Lutheran.' I was dumbfounded and could not respond ... all this time I thought they were both just Protestant Churches ... mine wasn't a Hindu temple. I couldn't get him to explain his feelings. On further reflection, however, I remembered some of the comments Joan has made over the months regarding her church and its policies ... Joan's church has slowly but surely been dying—falling apart. I have not studied the people of her church, but I think I can safely state the reason for its failure. If it is not true for her church, it can certainly be made applicable to the greater percentage of the American people today. Her church is old fashioned; it is narrow-minded; it has followed the line of conformity so long and so closely that today it is old and stale and rotting ... Neither the church nor the doctrine is rotting, it is the minds of the people who make it up that are decaying. They have nothing worthwhile to think about or keep their minds busy; so instead of turning to something good and constructive—and Christian, they let their minds decay with gossip, self-pity, self-centeredness and petty grievances. They are so busy with these things they have forgotten to love—to love their neighbor. They have convinced themselves that all they are doing is what is right—what their ancestors have taught them—what they have learned in church. And they are so sure they are right and good Christians they are afraid to step out of line and give airing to their own beliefs. This is not surprising, because they suppress, hide and destroy any thought of their own that even suggests there may be some parts of the system that could be wrong, or be done a better way. They are so engrossed in looking back, in trying to make themselves the same as their parents and grandparents that they have failed to make themselves individuals and failed to make a future for their own children.... Open the doors ... no, not the doors of the church, but the doors of your hearts. Let God come into your hearts and God is love. God is understanding and friendliness. God is setting yourself aside ..."

It doesn't matter what the denomination of her church, but it was the first time I'd discovered that not all Protestant churches thought alike, and not all congregations consisted of 'happy campers.' There might be a lot of 'glitter' around the pews, but not all was golden. This revelation didn't shake the foundations of my own beliefs; I was still a devout Christian—what ever *that* is.

When I now read some of the scribbling in those journals, I chuckle at the portent of things to come ... such as what I wrote on 26 June 1952 aboard the USNS Shanks (a troopship) on the way to the Philippines:

"... But I do not blame Joan; because somewhere in her childish adventures in love, she has come to believe that gentleness and weakness are one in the same. Joan wants to marry a *real man*. Ah, Joan, where did you acquire the conviction—though you love my broad shoulders and strong back—before I can be a *real man* I must have the mentality of an ape and the vocabulary of a truck driver (no offense to truck drivers.) ... Don't crush me, Joan; if I have anything good in me, bring it out, don't suppress it merely to keep alive in your mind a living example of what you want me to be, rather than what I really am ..."

I arrived back in the States from Clark Air Force Base, PI in February 1953, and by that time whatever had been between Joan and me had disappeared, leaving only a whisper of what might have been ...

what might have been a waste of two lives, especially when one considers where the future would carry my own mind and beliefs.

4

RENAISSANCE

The return to civilian life was difficult, but no more so than the first time I'd done it some three years before. Returning to civilian life is an instant step from one culture into another, where no one understands your language—the language of men bound together in a community of common purpose, common humor, common complaints, but most of all common understanding of a common world.

My brother, Don, invited me to live with his family and finish my degree at the University. of Toledo. I accepted, but when I stepped into the tiny farming community of Metamora, Ohio I could have been an alien for all practical purposes, and although I was welcome in the home of my oldest brother and his family, I could find no common ground on which to communicate—I'd come from another world, a world they could never comprehend or share. Their *family* was their world and I had yet to define a place in my own.

In the summer of 1953, between the Far East and returning to college, I began to think for myself. I'd been a good Christian until that time; I sang in the church choir, taught Sunday school, led a group of Boy Scouts, believed all the minister's sermons, etc., etc., etc. But then things began to change in my life. I'd read a newspaper article about a star—twenty-five light-years distant—that had exploded, and I began to ponder …

I pondered, 'That star might have had planets revolving around it, with people just like us living on them. A whole population may have disappeared twenty-five years ago, and we on Earth never knew—or cared. Those people had never heard of—nor were they saved by—Jesus, and so they were doomed to spend all eternity in hell. But, I reasoned, *There are millions of people on Earth who are born, live a lifetime and die—never having heard of Jesus. Will they all spend eternity in hell?* I rebelled, because *my* good and benevolent God would never allow this—something must be wrong ... I began to think and I began to doubt ... and in spite of the fear I'd had emblazoned in my psyche since childhood ... I was *not* struck by a bolt of lightning for doubting the *word*, and I had a new courage to explore ...

A friend loaned me a novel named, "High Valley." The story's locale was in Tibet, and it gave me my first exposure to Buddhism. I read the book as a Christian, and cringed at the 'stupidity' of those heathen Buddhists. I pushed on in my reading—and the story served to reinforce my own belief in the 'truths' I'd been taught from the Bible. The main character of the story was Chinese; a stranger who'd wandered into the valley and who viewed the 'ignorant Buddhist peasants' with much the same intolerance as myself. However, in the story, a Buddhist high monk spoke a line that opened my eyes—and its message remains with me to this day. He told the man from China ... "Your intolerance waives your right to an opinion." I was the Chinaman, and I had no right to an opinion about the most important aspect of my life ... *salvation.*

I questioned ...'History has witnessed the slaughter of millions of innocents in the name of religion, but what if two men kill each other in the name of their God—each believing he in the right and destined for paradise—who wins? If all religions profess the Truth, but they are all different ... who is right?'

I reasoned, 'Many religions are similar; some have the same ancient origins, but perhaps the common Truths have been lost over the centuries, or obscured or misunderstood. If I could study all of them—without intolerance—perhaps I might find that *fine thread of truth* that must weave throughout the tapestries of all religions.'

I sought answers by reading books by the great philosophers, but I found their mighty thoughts heavy with love of their own words, but little to fill my own yearnings for a logical path to Truth. Discussions with my Methodist minister, who was also a friend, contained my questions such as ... "Why do all the people who have never been saved—through no fault of their own—have to go to hell?" *Ooh, God makes special considerations for them, they will spend eternity with Jesus* ... My reaction was, "Ooh? Then why must *I* be perfect, just because I was born and raised in a Christian family?" *Well ... God acts in mysterious ways; we cannot expect to understand His reasons* ... Many questions were asked of 'learned men' and many answers were left wanting during that summer of searching; and the 'learned' men's knowledge was usually of a quality—'God acts in mysterious ways ...'

◆   ◆   ◆

I supported myself by working at an air conditioner manufacturing company during the summer after I returned from the Far East, and I enrolled in the University of Toledo with the intention of completing my engineering studies there. I took a quick trip back to Fort Wayne to renew old friendships, however, something happened there that made me change my mind about my future. When I visited Indiana Tech and walked into the bookstore, I was instantly remembered and welcomed by Nellie, the store manager. A few minutes later I chanced to meet the college president in the hallway; he smiled warmly, addressed me by name and welcomed me back from the wars. I knew, to attend the U. of Toledo, I'd be only one of thousands of students there ... an unknown among many unknowns. Although many of my friends had graduated from Tech by this time, I was back in familiar surroundings; I was *home.* I immediately changed my mind about where to complete my degree. It was also about this time I shifted my major/minor from Civil/Mechanical to Mechanical/Civil; I reasoned, a mechanical engineer could have more options when it came to making a living than an architect would.

In September, the friendly atmosphere, small student body and a large number of foreign students exposed me to many different cultures and religions. I soon had friends who were happy to discuss Confucius, Hinduism, Buddhism and the many variations of Christian beliefs. I'd learned if I showed an interest in someone's home country or culture they became instant friends. My engineering studies suffered, but it became the happiest period of my life.

◆   ◆   ◆

The 20 October 1953 entry in my journal relates the diverse path my mind started to take at this point in time …

"… A few months ago I began to question my Christian belief that through Christ is the *only* way to salvation. I am inclined to believe that our God—the only true God of the universe and maker of all things—is an all-wise and loving God; therefore, I do not believe He would restrict the possibility of acquiring salvation to only this planet, much less to only those few who have been exposed to the teachings of Jesus of Nazareth. I rather believe that all the sects of the Earth who worship one supreme deity all worship—in their own way—the same God. All sects worship the same God under different names, all have a savior but under a different name …"

I went on to expound more of my philosophy when I wrote …

"… Relative to the universe, a billion years is but a blink of an eye on the face of eternal time. What is a billion years but a mortal-given significance to a graduation of time, and relative only to mere mortal conception? If a billion years is merely man's graduation of time, how then does *God* graduate time? Or does He? Or in immortality, does time lose significance? If mortal life itself is only an infinitesimal segment of time—immortal life must be the absence of time. Before the existence of Earth there was time—therefore, the few billion years of the Earth too is infinitesimal. Wherein then, is the meaning of time? Is time and existence one in the same? (I had touched on a question here that had to wait many decades to be answered, and the meaning of time to be realized.)

"Before I was born I had a soul, I live, I have a soul and a body; when I die—as all living things must—and this body decays, I will still have a soul. If the soul is not mortal, can it be born with the mortal body, or does it die when the body is dead? If the soul is neither born nor dies, then the soul is immortal in a form—but if the soul is already immortal and I am unaware—then is *to be* aware—immortality? (Here I was probing the nature of the soul, a nature never having been defined by my religious teachers. I would have to stumble in darkness for many decades before I saw a light.)

"Omniscience! Ooh, would that my soul could leave this mortal body of sin and ignorance and dwell in the sublime beauty of Truth." (I considered Truth, with a capital 'T' as being one with God. But I also note, I still thought 'sin' inhabited my body.)

◆   ◆   ◆

I wrote a short Footprint that, in retrospect, astounds me with my insight ...

FOOTPRINTS: 3 December 1953

> "When the lamp of all knowledge
> burns brightly within the temple of the soul,
> why seek ye the light of wisdom
> out in the night of ignorance
> that is this world?"

I remember doing homework at my desk one Sunday afternoon in December; I paused, picked up a scrape sheet of paper and wrote on the back of it without stopping …

"My soul and God are one.
My soul findeth salvation through no man
Whether he be savior or incarnation;
I am my own salvation.

I shall not find God lest I find
My true self;
I find not my true self lest I search
Within myself.

I am not a book—nor is any book I,
Therefore, I cannot read myself.
I am not the world—nor is the world I,
Therefore, I cannot find myself in crowds.
I am not a star—nor is any star I,
Therefore, I cannot find myself in the universe.

When my flesh dies—my soul lives:
My flesh lives—my soul lives;
Before my flesh—my soul lives;
I cannot find myself in my flesh.

My true self is not flesh, nor book, nor world,
Nor universe—yet—
I am a part of all these
And all these are a part of me;
Where can I find my True Self if not within me?"

The wisdom expressed in that scribbling would not make an impression on anyone then or now, but what was unique at the time was the inspiration. I'd switched from calculus, and wrote without stopping or thinking; the words flowed out of my pen as though some other hand guided mine.

A few more words that flew from my pen in early 1954 and got recorded as FOOTPRINTS were ...

> "Oh children, be tolerant;
> With tolerance you many find understanding;
> With understanding you may find wisdom;
> With wisdom you may find truth;
> With truth you many find tranquility;
> With tranquility you may find meditation;
> With meditation you may find God;
> In God you will find immortality.
> Oh children, be tolerant."

> "Though what I know may be little,
> May what little I know be truth."

> "Religions were made by and for *man*;
> I seek salvation for my *soul*;
> What then can religions offer me
> But a shallow hiding place from fear?"

I must admit, not all my writing was *deep*; I wrote the little thing below about that time ...

> "A sparrow was sitting in the rain
> just outside my window pane.

Its coat was brown, its bill was black
The wind was ruff'ling up its back.

I threw my window open wide
And beckoned him to come inside.
He looked at me and blinked an eye
Then turned and flew into the sky.

I stood and stared into the gloom
And mused at length on life and tomb,
Till soft within my heart did sigh,
'We two are kin, that sparrow and I.'"

◆   ◆   ◆

It was during this time that I was introduced—how I don't remember—to the *Gospel of Ramakrishna* and the *Bhagavad-Gita*. In retrospect, I cannot imagine how I came upon some of the things I read. I'd had discussions with Hindu students, but the depth of their knowledge of philosophical Hinduism was comparable to the *philosophy* taught in our Christian Sunday Schools. I was interested in the philosophy of the *creators* of those religions, not the memories of storytellers who followed.

Time passed quickly in those days and although I studied, dated—and no doubt *thought*—I didn't always put my thoughts down on paper—however, it was in the spring of 1954 that I met Nila. Nila was a 'good' Christian, and although she was disturbed by some of my thoughts, she listened and asked questions. One of the questions and its answer were recorded in my 30 May 1954 journal ...

"Nila asked me last night, if there is so much truth to be learned in this world, why can't it be learned—why don't *you* teach it?" I could only answer, people do not like to believe truth when it challenges their sacred ignorance—and people do not want their sacred ignorance challenged. Christ preached truth 2000 years ago, but the world could not comprehend it then—nor can it now; the world would not accept it then—it will not now; the people crucified him then—they still crucify his message today by modifying it with their own desires. People will accept truth only so long as it is convenient to their desires—desires that reside in and below the stomach. Whenever someone tries to teach them or lead them in aspirations above and beyond the stomach—the heart and the mind—although they may follow for a while—they soon crucify him in one way or another; and it doesn't take his more serious followers long to start twisting and changing his teachings to fit more conveniently with their own desires—or as we might more subtly put it today—to coincide with progress and modern times—even though Truth is timeless.

"And then his 'devoted followers,' sit and argue among themselves, because they have differences of opinions as to what truths should be twisted in what way to meet what selfish desires—little knowing and little caring that from these desires stem all their miseries.

"It is little wonder then that truth has such a hard time fighting its way into a prominent position in our conscious world. In a world where we train to hate instead of love; where we work constantly to receive, instead of work to give; where those who show appreciation for some of the *finer* things in life are considered odd; where individualism is synonymous with eccentricity; and where the ignorant are called *hep* and the wise called *square*. Is it any wonder that truth has difficulties in being realized—and for those who seek it, difficulties in finding wives? (The slang for 'hep' and 'square' vary with time and place, but there will always be names used by those who glorify the ignorant and crucify the wise.)

"If there be truth for me to teach, let me teach; if there be ears to hear the truth, let them hear."

◆   ◆   ◆

I have been questioned about some of the things I wrote in my younger journals; I've been challenged and asked where I got the ideas or the *authority* to say the things I said. My answers to those questions ... 'I didn't *get* ideas. I didn't receive *authority*—I just wrote.' Many times I would be sitting at my desk doing homework and would suddenly reach for a piece of paper and start writing—often without pause—I would record words that flowed out of my pen, words that often did not pass through my brain ... Below is one such outpouring ...

"THE MIRROR AND THE POOL

"Upon looking into an old mirror, I find where the silver has peeled from the back, I can see through the glass and there is no reflection.

"I find some personalities are like old mirrors; if when looking into the eyes of a person I can see clear through them—like the glass—then I see their character is about as deep as the thin coating on the back of the mirror.

"But, people are like mirrors in other ways. Consider the basic property of a mirror—it reflects what is placed in front of it; that is all it can do. A pool may also reflect an image, but unlike the mirror, reflection is not its only property. The pool not only reflects beauty, but it has beauty of its own. With the passing of time, the mirror loses even borrowed beauty; but the pool retains and even adds. Break the surface of the mirror and the beauty is broken forever; break the surface of the pool and only the surface is disturbed, and soon it is normal again—yes, and even in the disturbed surface, there is a simple beauty in the moving of the water—and deep within the pool there is a serenity that even the most wild winds cannot move. The same storms that cause great oceans and rivers to rage, cause but simple ripples upon the surface of the pool."

"At the pool's edge flowers grow, and to those who would thirst, the pool will give drink; and though the surface may be hidden, those who seek truth simply brush debris aside and learn—the pool itself is beauty.

"In this world, there are people who are mirrors and there are people who are pools. Some reflect beauty; others are beauty itself. Place some in gaiety and they are gay; others bring their joy from within. Expose some to triumph or disaster and they reflect the same; others show but simple ripples over depths of tranquility.

"Too often in our search for beauty in people, we seek out the shiny surfaced mirrors and pass by those hidden pools—whose only need is for someone to brush aside their surface shroud—and let beauty itself shine forth."

◆   ◆   ◆

It was on 10 June 1954 when I *listened* to my 'Voice' for the first time. The incident was recorded in detail on the pages of my journal, but I'll be brief here ... Nila and I had been dating for a while, and had talked at length about life and death and God—a favorite subject of mine. I had talked with her for awhile on the phone this particular evening; afterwards I sat at my desk pondering our new relationship. All my previous girlfriends had come along just at a time when I needed them to save me from a pit of depression—of one kind or another—but then in time we had gone our separate ways. This night I questioned, 'I'm facing no crisis at this time; why has Nila come into my life?' A clear voice spoke within me, "Nila is not here for you; you are here for her. Her father will die tonight." Nila's father died of a heart attack at approximately the same time as the Voice spoke to me. I wasn't told of her father's death until late the next day—but when I was told—all I could say was, "I know." It shocked me that I had known with such certainty of his death, even before it happened.

I called Nila right after learning, and I wrote in my journal of the call …

"Nila and her mother are taking it very well. Nila said that I had prepared her for it with my talks of death, souls, etc., and her father's death wasn't so bad now."

And later I wrote, "Today I went to the funeral, and now I sit and wonder … I walk in a mist, alone, walking to no known destination, for no known reason, just wandering and wondering, 'Why?'"

In time, Nila and I went our separate ways, but in the parting-pages of my Nila-journal, I wrote …

"So how does it go, in order to have a happy modern love with a modern girl in a modern society, you must play the *game* and fall into the long narrow line of conformity. You must give up the few virtues taught to you in Sunday school and take on the popular dogmas of the masses. Not necessary are common loves with your wife, but common hates; not common interests, but common prejudices; not lovers of truth, but seekers of convention. And when you have this, what have you? Nothing! Drink from the cup of life and when you have drunk all—what have you? Nothing! Fill the cup of life with all it will hold and even more than it can hold, what have you? Nothing! Only in the *freedom* from all these does one really find *Something* …

> "Who cares to seek
> For that perfect freedom?
> One man, perhaps,
> In many thousands.
> Then tell me, how many
> Of those who seek freedom
> Shall know the total
> Truth of my being?

Perhaps one only."
(Bhagavad-Gita)

◆   ◆   ◆

I expected to graduate in August of 1955, but scheduling conflicts that summer term made it necessary to remain another term to get my degree. My new job at RCA would have to wait—and it did. The summer found me exchanging ideas with a woman who worked at the college. Some discussions took place over an occasional lunch, but for the most part we exchanged ideas through short notes. We shall call her "Oottie," which was the nickname I gave her.

She was married, but found no soul mate in her husband (Please forgive my use of the term 'soul mate;' it has yet to be defined to my satisfaction.) She was thirteen years my senior, but we enjoyed communicating on many different levels of thought, and she became a 'sounding board' for my immerging divergent ideas. The relationship evolved quickly into a form of love—not a sexual love—but a strong desire to share and enjoy each other's thoughts and company. I still have some of the notes I sent to her, and it perhaps it would be clarifying if I could put those notes in some semblance of order but, on these fifty-year-old slips of paper, neither the dates nor the inspiration for the writing is evident; so I will just spread them out here and let my loving reader gently blow away the chaff from the grain …

I wrote this to her in June 1955 …

"THE PLIGHT OF THE INDIVIDUAL

"If one is to be a true individualist, let it be only because of the road he travels alone, not a goal he seeks. A person who roams the lofty meadows of thought must indeed walk alone most of the time, for few there be whom he will meet there. By virtue of his uniqueness he becomes an individualist.

"Who cares to walk constantly alone? Not many, and for those who attempt to do so, the conflict with convention and opposition can be miserably frustrating. The extent and effect of this initial frustration may determine a life lost or a life lived.

"The greatest frustration presents itself in the overcoming of inertia; inertia that can be attributed to the various ties we possess in this massive illusion we call 'life.' These 'ties' consist mainly of duties to family, spouse and friends. True, duty must be met with performance, but to most of the performers, the line of duty loses definition under the wear of the ego and self-pitying martyrdom. The human mind contracts and expands the boundaries of duty in accordance with personal desires. Duty, rightly performed, in the absence of ego and without concern for results, can be an aid rather than a hindrance to the aspirant in his journey along the path to Truth.

"The person who aspires to the 'Path' but finds himself caught in the strangling web of conformance for conformance sake and convention for convention's sake is miserable indeed. The possession of material things, and activities that bring conventional happiness to others, leave the aspirant in a void. The security brought by conventional success and accepted religion, leave him insecure and empty. He is like a person lost in the jungle, knowing that within a few feet there is a wide path to home, but knowing not in what direction to look he gets deeper, always deeper into the jungle. Oh, for someone to point the way. '… Many there be who have need of thee, but few there be who will call.'

"The first step in the direction of freedom, the first expression of the desire to break the bonds of the 'jungle of delusion,' sets the seeker apart from the floundering masses. He then becomes—to the orthodox—an eccentric, a dreamer, an escapist—and if not ostracized then he is pitied—a person to be humored, but not understood.

"The weak aspirant cannot withstand the condemnation of society, and soon returns to that long narrow line of conformity. And when he is back in his little 'square box' (as you call it), containing his infinitesimal world, it will be said of him, 'Oh, he had funny ideas once, but he out-grew them.' And to him the 'box' is more empty than before, the jungle thicker and his happiness more superficial.

"The seeker that is strong and resists the initial onslaught of society, grows stronger with the acquisition of discrimination; then he sees truly who is the dreamer and who the escapist. Through discrimination he develops a sense of the relative value of things, and finds all 'things' valueless, the 'constant' mutable, and all existence transitory.

"'... Decay is inherent in all living things; work out your salvation with diligence.'

"The aspirant who realizes this learns there is only one Reality, only One that is not transient. He who seeks this Divine Reality, without concern for 'what will be thought of me,' or 'whom will I hurt,' forsaking *all,* he will find the only true Happiness, the only Existence.

"'But what of my family,' you ask, 'what of my little square box full of duty, obligation and compliance with custom? Surely one cannot forsake all these for selfish ends' ... And when your body decays and dies, where then is your family, your duty to man, your obligation to custom? Seek that which is Real, all else slips through the fingers like grains of sand and are lost forever in the ocean of time. The five billion years of Earth are but a blink of an eyelash on the face of eternal time; how real then are our petty lives? As real as an unseen wave breaking on an unknown shore, as real as a forgotten cloud drifting in a forgotten summer sky, as real as last night's dream ... no more. Seek that which has worth.

"'... He that would come after me, let him take up his cross and follow me.'

"Little one, where is your faith? Do you think that God, in all His wisdom cannot solve your simple problems? Why do you say, 'But ...'"

Ootie wanted to walk the *Lonely Road*, but she was torn between obligations to a marriage and her desire to 'soar with eagles.' We continued to share our thoughts and ideas throughout that long hot summer. Below is another one of my thoughts that I shared with her ...

"FOOTPRINTS:

The Ego

"It is hard to conceive a person existing without an ego. The ego has become so much a part of our lives and thinking that for all common purposes, we *are* our ego. So much are we our ego that an attempt to alienate it from our actions would require an effort of considerable magnitude.

"In present day terminology, the ego is normally considered to be an evil possessed only by the egotistical. Even the dictionary supports popular ignorance in maintaining this fallacy. The dictionary combines the body and the soul under the ego, whereas in reality, it is the ego that blinds us to the true nature of the soul.

"Before anything worthwhile can be attained, either materially or spiritually, the ego much be eliminated from our every thought, action and aspiration. Until this elimination is accomplished, a true and lasting happiness can never be attained, for it is from this ego—from which stems desire—that *all* our miseries spring. Prove me wrong—if you can.

"To the person seeking happiness as a goal in itself, happiness will never come, for the seeking itself is inspired by the ego. *Happiness is merely a by-product—an ornament that adorns the vehicle (our body) we drive down the road to enlightenment (Truth).*

"One of the first obstructions we must surmount on this 'road' is the elimination of this ego. The first step toward elimination must be in having a profound will to eliminate it; without this there is no need of starting, because to those who fear the truth, there are many heartaches. Many, nay, nearly all of our age-old cherished and even sacred beliefs will be challenged and changed. The traveler must cast aside his cloak of ego-rationalization and take up the sword of pure discrimination.

> '.... Where is your sword
> Discrimination?
> Draw it and slash
> Delusion to pieces ...'"

I was writing here about the delusion that makes us think our ego is our true self. What *is* our true self? There's the rub, is it not why we are here in this lifetime ... to *remember?* It is not a quest of *finding*; it is a case of *remembering.*

I was beset by a fire and brimstone sermon during that summer and it inspired the following ...

FOOTPRINTS:

"If, for religion's sake, we condemn anything, we should not err by giving misguided reasons for the condemnation, or the slightest inquiring mind will find the fallacy and be either confused or put in doubt about the whole religion.

"In modern religions, condemnations are farces in that neither the condemners nor the abstainers know the true reasons for their actions.

"The condemners hide behind the scriptures they do not comprehend and the abstainers merely follow like cattle, feeling safe and content to be lead from darkness to darkness.

"'Go out into the darkness and put your hand into the hand of God, and that, for you, will be better than a lamp and safer than a known way.' But do not deify the wrong thing; there is but one God. One may consider the scriptures as a 'lamp' and the *only way* the 'known way.' In the hands of God *only* are you truly safe"

◆   ◆   ◆

I always needed to work at part-time jobs while in school, often having to change jobs to accommodate conflicting class schedules. I found a new job servicing G.E. appliances for a local distributor. This job offered experiences I'd never imagined. I serviced appliances in all strata of Fort Wayne society, and I was exposed to a wide variation of homes and housekeeping. I'd always known middle class Mid-western homes, all maintained by reasonably neat and clean people. I learned that houses—like people—'what you see on the outside doesn't necessarily reflect what's on the inside.'

Oottie and I continued to share our reflections around my new schedules, such as when I wrote the following ...

"You asked me, 'Can one worship and still not go to church?'

"Let us consider how we worship in church ... We must not worship an idol, but we kneel before the cross ... but, you say, it is not the act but the state of mind while kneeling that is important. We sing a hymn, mumble over our beads, read the Bible and many other things, but it is *not* the action that is important, it is the state of mind. The mind must be in a state of worshiping God.

"Well then, if the action is not important, then the state of mind must be *all* important. If the state of mind is all-important then the action could be anything or nothing at all.

"If the mind is in a state of worship, then the body can be in an act of doing anything, whether it be kneeling before an idol, walking, typing, cooking, fishing or anything at all. Therefore, if our mind is fixed on God, our every daily action—large or small—becomes an act of worship.

"If the mind is fixed on God, we do our duty, live our lives and pass among objects, but know neither attraction (from which springs attachment) nor aversion for those objects, because our mind is on God.

"When we can pass among objects and know neither attraction nor aversion, we will know tranquility.

"Can we worship and still not go to church? When God dwells within the temple of the soul, how much more can we find in a church?"

FOOTPRINTS:
"Jesus said, 'Be ye perfect as your Father in heaven is perfect.' But I am taught that I am a sinner, born in sin, imperfect and can be nothing else—even if I accept Jesus as my savior. If I must be perfect to enter heaven, but can never be perfect, what hope have I?'"

FOOTPRINTS:
"In the book of John it is written that Jesus said, "… I am the Way … no man cometh unto the Father but by me." (This can be found *only* in the book of John.) This, in my mind, is inconsistent with the rest of His teachings, if taken literally—which in most cases it is—for he also said, 'Seek ye first the kingdom of heaven …' and that 'The kingdom of heaven is within you.' All great religions and philosophies teach the last part, but only one little statement (I am the way …) teaches the other. If the kingdom of heaven is within me, why must I be saved by something or someone outside of me? Why must I accept someone as my 'savior?'"

Our friendship eventually evolved into somewhat more than being 'just friends;' though it never progressed beyond the kissing stage. It was frustrating for her, to be bound to a marriage and its obligations, while having a mind that wanted to soar as an individual. Our minds soared together, but we were still tethered to the Earth-bound world of reality, which no doubt inspired the following …

FOOTPRINTS:

"'What is so rare as a day in June?' A true friendship. What is a true friendship? Is a true friendship possible between two people of the opposite sex?

"It seems when two people fall in 'love,' their relations cease to be that of a blending of two minds to that of a mixing of two egos—the two egos, consisting of two ideologies and the egos—complete with all the selfish temperaments and desires—then create a battlefield. Hence, the minds can no longer soar on a level of ideals, but must grope through the jungle of appeasement, conformity and subsistence.

"To those who realize the fall from the high, frustration follows, but there are so few marriages that begin on the higher level that it is hardly worth considering. Many books have been written about survival in the 'jungles' of the lower level, but what of the survival or return of those fallen few? Is there a return for those who see things as they are and long to return to the road of Reality?"

And later I wrote to her ...

"... This is a crazy, mixed-up life isn't it; a guy could write a book about it. But you know, every little thing has its lesson, every episode, every situation—even ours—we've just got to keep on pushing and looking for the lesson. If we look for the *good* in everything that happens—it's always there—we can find that lesson. Usually it isn't until it's all over that we see the true light. We've just got to keep looking for that good side, Oottie. Even *our* difficulties have their function if you look for the good. I don't know just how, but the reasons are there and we'll find them. Every little grain of sand has its part of the hour, every stroke of the brush its part of the painting, and every note its part in the symphony; *our* frustrations and our happiness too have their part in the 'big picture.' Just like a jig-saw puzzle, the parts may not fit at first, but with patience and faith in the Maker, they fit sooner or later. Our parts will fit too, Oottie, and no matter what the final picture is, it is for the best—wait and see. Our parts all seem so large, so important, but ...

"'... they are of such great importance only as they pass from the upper to the lower glass; although insignificant there in the lower glass, the hour is not complete without them, and without the hour-glass there is still time'"

In retrospect, this was not the first nor would it be the last time a platonic relationship would evolve into something different. A woman with whom I might find a common desire to exchange ideas, would become more interested in my body than my mind. I must always chuckle when I hear a woman utter a comment of disgust, 'Men are only interested in a woman's body, they don't care if she has a mind.' I've never been aware of a stranger 'lusting after my body,' but neither was I ever aware of a woman wondering if I had a brain. We are only human, and humans follow their natural inclinations—and, Lord knows, I am no exception—I always hoped for just a little more in a woman than animal attraction.

I wrote to Ottie on 22 July 1955 ...

"... I have a lot of ideas about wives and families that are perhaps too idealistic, but that old worn phrase that 'No one is perfect,' just isn't accepted by me. A person says that, and he or she thinks that justifies all their many faults—or as one girlfriend put it—'that's the way I am, that's the way God wants me to be, so what can I do ...' I say a person *can* be perfect, but it doesn't come easy, it takes years—even lives—of honest effort and prayer. The person may never reach perfection, but what's the difference, even if he *tries* he'll be a way out front. Set your goal low and even if you attain it, you have nothing; set your goal among the stars and even if you fail you'll still be among the highest.

"I set my goal among the stars and began to pray for an understanding heart; by and by it came to me that goals in themselves are transient, the striving unimportant, and that there is only one Goal worth
striving for, and He is the Goal, the Striving and the Striver ... I am
the striver and I am Him; knowing this, my goal is no longer the stars,
they are my home."

The last note I wrote to Oottie before she left Fort Wayne was written on 31 July 1955 ...

"I am so glad to have found so fine a friend as you; a person with
whom I could talk, and give and receive friendship in return. I can
withdraw into my secret closet and love you, and still not be frustrated
by not having or hoping for love in return. I wrote to you on a philosophical plane and had my writing received, enjoyed and even understood. I brought you books to read and, much to my amazement, you
read them and enjoyed them.

"I'd found someone who must have liked to hear me talk—not just
tolerating my jabbering until I was maneuvered into a 'hooking' position. You couldn't fall in love with me, so you must have actually
enjoyed me. You inspired me to think and to write and to read and I
loved you for it. I would not allow myself to dwell on thoughts of loving you on a physical or passionate plane—I had no right. I had no
right to love you in deed, therefore not in thought. When I found out
you loved me, I was quite bewildered—not frustrated—just walking
on unfamiliar ground.

"Our talking and writing—and my thinking—left the philosophical
plane and stepped down into the streets of everyday living—that is, we
were no longer two dear friends sipping leisurely from our tea cups and
enjoying each other's company; but we became two lovers grasping,
draining each drop—each moment—from the 'cup,' and feeling
cheated when there was no more—and knowing that too soon there
would be no re-fill. Desperation tended to make us cleave too strongly

to what was fleeting—time—and dread too much the future. Desperation made us forget the joy of the past and fail to realize that the source of that joy was being neglected.

"You asked if you have lost me and destroyed our closeness ... Nay, we have merely forgotten where we put it; all we need do is pick it up again.

"And what of tomorrow, can we just let our love drop, and go on as though nothing has passed between us?

"Tomorrow is not important, nor today, nor yesterday. Yesterday is memory, today is an illusion and if tomorrow never comes ... what difference? Should I step down to worrying about tomorrow and lose some of that virtue for which you love me?

"If you really love me, the greatest way you can show it is by upholding those things in which we believe. Accept what is given to you and treat it as it is the Giver. Be free in your mind and no man can bind you. Learn to love wisely and forget how to hate ..."

Oottie left Fort Wayne and I was alone again, walking the lonely road and hoping to find someone with whom I could exchange ideas. Our minds had soared together, but then she, too, became part of the past. I graduated in November 1955 and strode on into the future of my engineering career.

5

A CAREER

Radio Corporation of America in Findlay, Ohio, received the 'bless-ings' of my first tentative steps into the corporate world. It was also a time and place when I began to wonder why I'd chosen the field of engineering—I wasn't happy. Well, not true, I liked the field of engi-neering, but what I hated was the field of corporate politics. I had stormed into that world with a B.S.M.E. degree in my hand and thought 'I had the world by the tail.' In reality, I didn't know squat! I didn't know that a college degree only meant I'd received passing grades at some college or university; it didn't guarantee I'd learned any-thing. I made friends, mostly men with whom I worked—it's not that I didn't like the girls in Findlay—I figured they just didn't like *me*. I don't recall having even one real date in that town. In retrospect, I had numerous friends, but they were all married and there seemed to be no context in which I could meet single women. I resorted to traveling back to Ft. Wayne on weekends to mix with established friends. In 1956 there were no apartment complexes in Findlay, and furnished apartments for bachelors were hard to find, so I purchased a new forty-four foot, two-bedroom house trailer. (That was a *big* trailer in those days.) It turned out to be a good investment.

A few thoughts reflected during that period were such as written on 27 February 1956 …

"FOOTPRINTS:

"There is no death; nothing is finite because of its duration. The universe is merely a state of matter that is in constant change. Our universe—which is all we perceive—is but an infinitesimal segment of time, a grain of sand in the hourglass of time-infinite. The universe is only as large or as small as we ourselves. We ourselves can be infinitesimal or infinite.

"We ourselves and our universe—perceived or unperceived—are but a small part of an everlasting cycle. Some laugh at reincarnation, but the very food we live on is something that once lived, and lived because of something which lived before it and nourished its growth—in its own part of the 'cycle.' We are a part of the universe and the universe is part of us, only the cycle changes and we take on our different state or office. The 'cycle' is a continuous form of decay; whether we are animal, plant or mineral we are still part of the universe, and we too soon have our change of state.

"But if we are part of infinity and there is only one Infinite, then we must be one and the same with that Infinite—whether we be in any state of change—human, plant or mineral—all is God. How wonderfully simple it all is."

On 1 October 1956 I reflected on the strong pull and yearnings that autumn always brought to me …

"It is autumn again; the leaves are dressing for their last glory and soon they shall return to time, their cycle completed. The smell of their burning lends punctuation to the beauty of the season—and it *is* beautiful. I have always loved the fall; loved it even though it always brings a certain longing—or rather perhaps a yearning. As I consider the yearning, I know not its object—perhaps the woodlands and hills of home; but even as a boy a strange emptiness thrust itself upon me with the first frost, an emptiness that longed to be filled. What is this thing for which I yearn when the Mallards gather and turn south? What draws me into the dark blue sky to join the cirrus cloud—a solitary brushstroke in that vast emptiness? That azure blue through which the warm sun rushes to lend a golden beauty to the rustling stacks of corn as they stand in the field—waiting."

I attended a homecoming at Tech that fall and bumped into an old classmate who worked in the Engine Design Department at GMC Truck & Coach Division in Pontiac, Michigan. I didn't hesitate one second to accept his invitation to 'come up and look us over.' My corporate learning experience with RCA lasted exactly one year.

◆   ◆   ◆

General Motors opened up new horizons for me. I was paired with an older engineer whose patience and guidance made me realize that my education didn't mean a thing if I didn't make it produce something by working with people. As an engine design engineer I worked with many departments and levels of the corporation—I belonged—and it was a feeling I'd never experienced at RCA.

I learned too that towns and cities are different. I had accepted my first position with RCA because it was in a small town—I was a small town boy. I believed that small towns are, by nature, friendlier and I'd make many new friends—I was wrong. In Pontiac, after having been exposed to two small towns and two large cities in a period of five years, I came to the conclusion that small towns might be friendly to strangers, but then you must *prove* yourself to become a friend. Large cities may not be friendly to strangers, but because many of the people you meet came there as strangers themselves, they tend to accept you for just what you are—another person. Small town people, I found, don't need new friends, they've grown up with the ones they have; I guess they don't need or want any more.

In Pontiac, I became involved with a youth group from a Methodist church, sang in the choir (I liked to sing ... and the choir had *girls*.) It appears from my journals, however, I was still lonely for companionship, and I dreamed of a woman—and in my loneliness I wrote ...

"Oh, for a woman that would help me to realize what I am—who would let me be myself and love me for the me I am, rather than the person she wants me to be. I want in this life to strive toward perfection in myself, but I need a woman who knows in what direction perfection lies, and understands my striving and loves me for that. I think the only woman that could fulfill all these things is one who herself is striving to rise above 'here and now and all trivia.' I have been told that I am too particular—a 'perfectionist.' Well, perhaps, but then what is perfection? In the land of the blind, the one-eyed man is king."

I have written very little herein of the women in my life, because this book is intended to relate and reflect on the years and thoughts that brought me to my present philosophical leanings. It is evident however, that we all have an impact on the lives of others, and others have their impact on ours, and although their touch may be soft as a breeze or violent as a tempest, they nudge us in our direction down the path we travel. Barbara was one such person in my life. She caused great turmoil, but she also brought a whisper of love and softness when it was needed, and although she was seven years younger than I, this young woman brought much beauty into my life. I met her about a month after I arrived in Pontiac, and within a short time I became mind-entangled over her. I wrote a 'Portrait' of her in my journal ...

"A small dimly-lit living room is crowded with people sitting in various types of chairs, waiting for color slides to be projected upon a white screen before them. Across the room from where I sit is a closed door—a quiet knock, the door is opened—a soft mellow feminine voice tiptoes into the room with a greeting and is silent. Later, the 'voice' moves to a small stool in front of where I sit—I tap her on the shoulder and offer my chair, she smiles and accepts. In time, introductions are made and I meet Barbara Kline.

"A soft pleasant voice, eyes that look into mine when we talked and I desired to know them again. This is the portrait of Barbara that I carried from that room in January 1957."

I should explain to my reader, it was a habit of mine to relate in my journal about any new girl who arrived on my scene; I wanted to record raw first impressions, in case our relationship developed into something worthy of note. There were many women who touched my life briefly, and I never saw them again. I mention only those who had an impact on my emotions or added measurably to my progress along the *path*. Barbara was one such person, and she deserves a prominent place in this history. I'll continue with the my early writings about her …

"After two months of an acquaintance, I can sum it up very shortly—Barbara is potentially a mature woman—but I don't trust her. This distrust has plagued me for months and I still do not understand. Perhaps it is because I regard her as somewhat unique—her apparent interest in and ability to understand Eastern philosophy has set her apart from the crowd. Her obvious keen perception exhibited in our discussions has helped keep her in that light, but she is not all individual—other things she does put her right back with other masses of … I have been trying to understand her in the light of her individuality, when the greatest percentage of her is in the darkness of the herd. It is very much like a jigsaw puzzle—I am trying to put all the pieces together when only a few of the pieces are turned upright. As it is, none of the pieces fit together. I guess the only solution is to consider first those pieces which are in the majority and see if I can at least establish a pattern—we shall see."

In April I came down with the flu and the effects on my mind and writing are evident in the following:

"My mind is in chaos; I am sick in my body, and being home alone all day has made me sick of myself. I think I will put on Tchaikovsky's Symphony Number Six; it will be very appropriate for my state of mind ...

"My body is still ill, but my mind is a little clearer. I sometimes forget the power of music to quiet a restless mind.

"It isn't very often I find a girl I could love; I may find one who holds my curiosity for a while, but soon she falls by the wayside, unable to fill that void in me which longs to be filled. Perhaps I've hurt some girls in the past because of this void—I've shown them attention, got them excited, then in time I go my way—alone. I never told them I loved them, never wanted to imply anything more than friendship. If I've hurt them I'm sorry, but ...

"Barbara may be a girl who can fill that void. She is young, but she has a keen perception and a depth of which I believe she is not aware. I have given her a little of myself, to let her know that I exist. If she has a need of me, then I am here and will take her into my heart; if she finds no need of me then I will go my own way—a little richer.

"And now this sick mass of flesh of mine needs sleep."

The next day, I obviously was feeling no better when I wrote ...

"The least of my fears is death. Sometimes I think that death would be sweet. Sometimes I just get tired of living, and if my affairs weren't in such a sorry state, maybe I'd shoot myself. I'm not worth a damn. If I could take all the things in which I excel and piled them in a heap, they wouldn't even be visible. I say I'm an engineer—Ha! I'm a stupid ass. I think I can write—Ha! I'm too lazy to write a letter, much less a book—and I couldn't anyway. I think I know God—I am nothing but a fool. A fool who sheds tears in self-pity and thinks they are tears of longing for God.

"I'm a dreamer, a fake, an egoist, but I am sick, and I have no doctor … I have no one to whom I can talk.

"I think I am falling in love with Barbara—I don't want to fall in love with her. I feel she has rejected me … I'm too old, too silly, too serious, too dead, too ugly, too much wrapped up in myself.

"All I want to be is myself; won't somebody accept me as I am or what I want to be … Who wants an ass when they can buy a car? Oh to hell with it."

Still not fully recovered, I had ventured out among people and later wrote …

"The chaos of mind returns.

"The knowledge of my ignorance and stupidity makes me weep bitter tears. How simple it would be to clear my mind of all its chaos—as simple as pulling a trigger.

"I see too much and I see too deeply, and the stupidity—the pettiness of life—the damned triviality of it all drives me insane. But in spite of the subjects of my frustration and chaos, I know the cause of it all is Barbara. Although I have nothing against her, my frustration over her is what causes the winds of my restless mind to rage in protest at the world.

"Oh God, take me Home. I grow so weary of this world. I am so sick of this mass of flesh I call 'me,' which is choking my soul."

On 14 April 1957 I wrote …

"I'm twenty-eight years old now. How about that."

The months passed, Barbara and I dated and spent many hours together talking and enjoying each other. We had our times of hot and cold relations, but the more we learned of each other the more we knew we wanted to spend our lives together. We became engaged and set a wedding date of 18 January 1958.

In reading my journal now and using nearly fifty more years of maturity, I can see what probably caused the conflicts we had. Although she was about seven years younger than I, in many ways she was more mature in the realm of a love relationship. I will not go into details, because it is not the purpose of this book, but it is with sadness—not regret, but sadness of my ignorance—that I now read and understand the events of those days. I took a walk one day, while in one of my depression-depths, and afterwards wrote this ...

"I went for a walk in the woods today, my heart was heavy, my mind was restless and I was alone. I walked a long way through the signs of autumn; the sun shown warmly, but I was cold in my heart. The woods and fields were at peace, but in my being raged a war of hate and fear and jealously, and I cried unto the Lord asking,

"'God, why have you left me?' But my ears were deaf.

"I walked on and on, and as I walked the dusty road I asked, 'Oh God, am I alone?' And a voice within me spoke saying,

"'See that little wild flower hidden in the grass there—is it alone?'

"And I said, 'No it isn't, God is there.'

"And the voice asked, 'See that little grasshopper there—it hops and I am its hopping and I am each blade of grass it leaves and to each it jumps. Is it alone?'

"And I said 'No, it is not a lone.

"And the voice spoke saying, 'and if I am with all these little things, would I leave you alone?'

"And I said, 'No, Lord, I am not alone.'

"And the voice said, 'I am the before, the during and the after of all things, now and evermore; know me in thy self and in all things, and you will never be alone. Now go up unto that hill and listen for the voice of God.'

"I went up unto the hill where the sun filtered down through the trees and warmed the ground beneath, and I sat and listened. And I heard His voice in the wind as it whispered through the trees; and I heard His voice in the song of the birds as they fluttered to and fro. I heard His voice in the falling leaves as they wafted down to earth. And I listened. And I cried unto God asking, 'What should I do, oh Lord?'

"A voice spoke to me saying, 'Turn thy wrath from Barbara, turn thy wrath from Barbara, turn thy wrath from Barbara. Give to her your pure love and your faith; nothing can be solved with hate and distrust. For the entire universe I have a plan, and each thing is a part of that plan. *You* are a part of that plan—and Barbara. Have faith and fear not, for I will guide your way. Have faith. Go therefore, and turn your wrath from Barbara and from Barbara's mother and from Blair, love them; for though you think they hurt you, they are my children just as you, my son. Go now, in love and in peace; bathe and go to Barbara for she has need of your strength. Take a leaf from this tree—pure and free—as a symbol of your love.'

"And I took a leaf and as I walked, I picked wild flowers and red leaves that Barbara might share my walk in the woods with God."

This was the second time I listened to the Voice, the voice I now know speaks to all of us—we just don't listen.

January came and went and we did not marry. Barbara called the engagement off and later that same year she married the 'Blair' referred to above. Our parting was not in pain—it was inevitable. Although my journal of those months shows much turmoil of mind, I came away from the romance a much wiser person and carried no bitterness. A young woman opened my eyes to a beauty to which I'd been blind. I'd never heard of Kahlil Gibran until Barbara introduced me to THE PROPHET; a gift for which I have always been deeply grateful. Barbara was wise beyond her years, wiser by far than I in many ways. I now wonder if she ever found that which we both sought—back then—so many eons ago.

◆   ◆   ◆

In time I joined the Civil Air Patrol, took up downhill skiing and started a ski club. There were lonely times and times of companionship; there were new friends and new growth in professional skills, and too, growth in the social graces—many of which had been sorely lacking in my education. There was still the searching however, always the emptiness longing to be filled—emptiness I could never define. I suspect I was *not* alone in an empty life, because I wrote one Sunday—after attending a drunken brawl of singles the night before ...

"We all live in our own little worlds, and the objects in those worlds are only so big or so small as the meaning we ourselves give to them. I think about the people last night, and say to myself ... 'How crammed full of nothing their lives must be, so young, so empty ... And even when they grow older, how full of worth will their lives be? They have nothing today but the party last night, and the party next Saturday night. Their week is six books with empty pages, held upright by Saturday 'bookends.'"

I had an article published in The Detroit Times in March of 1959; it indicates I sometime thought about something other than my loneliness. It follows ...

"In a recent article written by an automotive executive, he indicated that by increasing the number of inspectors and inspections in the manufacturing process, he could bring the quality of workmanship in his product up to the standard found in European automobiles. All I can say to him is, 'Good Luck.'

"What this manufacturer failed to mention is that increased quality control means increased rejects, increased rejects mean increased rework and scrap, increased quality control, rework and scrap mean increased costs, and we all know that increased cost does not necessarily mean increased quality. You cannot inspect quality into a product; you must build it in.

"Built-in quality comes from only one place—the individual worker. An engineer can design his heart-out on the drawing board to produce a superior product on paper, but if the man on the production line has no pride in his own workmanship, then the engineer might just as well have stayed home. His superior product is going to be rejected at inspection—or go out onto the market as scrap, which is just what a large percentage of today's products are.

"Pride in workmanship is nearly a lost virtue in American industry today. Pride in individual workmanship requires an individual, and in today's industry a man is no longer an individual; he is a clock number, a position on the line, a union classification—but not an individual human being.

"Rather than recognition as an individual, he is given a six cent raise (after losing two months wages striking for it) or given this benefit or that material consolation. The result is, in spite of what his high wages can buy him and what security his fringe benefits can give him, the American worker is basically unhappy in his job.

"Who is to blame for the worker's unhappiness? Management? The Union? Why not blame it on Sputnik, everything else is. Blame anybody or anything, but don't blame yourself—you the reader.

"Instead of sitting around pointing fingers at the other guy, let's all do something about it. Let's recognize the individual as such and make him aware that he is recognized. But is this so easily done?

"Let's say that a certain man—new on the job—takes pride in his workmanship, so instead of putting a banged-up door panel on a car, he lays it aside and installs a good one, thus eliminating the necessity of replacing it at the end of the line. Or instead of leaving the stripped threaded bolt in the frame, he puts in a new bolt so that the car will stay together long enough for someone to buy it—and even consider buying the new model next year. Let's say that this worker—taking pride in his workmanship—decides to give his employer an honest day's work for an honest day's pay. First, he must overcome the fear of being an outcast; he runs the risk of being called a 'company man' or a 'brown nose,' because it is the popular philosophy of today to get just as much as you can for nothing in return. If, in spite of opposition from the crowd, he decides to do a good job and—if he has a good foreman—might be recognized as a good worker, what can the foreman do to reward him? Give him a raise? No, sorry; his Union Classification doesn't allow it. Then let's give him a better job—no, sorry, he doesn't have enough seniority. How long will a man produce superior work with only a pat on the back? Soon he joins the crowd and its attitude of 'to hell with the company and hurray for me;' And another individual is lost to a system geared to coddle the *inferior* worker and suppress the *superior* worker.

"Here, in a nut shell, is the decline and fall of the American way of life. Suppress a man's right and desire to be an individual; glorify the idea of getting everything for nothing; couple this with the present apathy of the masses, and you have a perfect formula for destruction. We have taken the formula and are running joyously down the path to extinction as a free people. Don't waste your H-bombs, Russia; be patient, and the American people will beg you to show them your way to slavery."

A half-century has passed since I wrote that article; relations with Russia have improved, but the 'American way of life' has not.

◆   ◆   ◆

Eventually I met and 'went steady' with another woman—another Barbara. We were in love for a time, but then something happened which I do not understand to this day. I wrote about it in my journal ...

"... For some reason or other, on that day back in May of '59, I fell out of love with Barb. I have racked my brain ever since trying to determine why. Before that day, I thought we had a close communication, sort of an unspoken understanding of one another—or at least she of me. (I question my understanding of *any* woman.) I learned on that day that most of what I discussed with her went right over her head—she didn't 'dig' me at all; she was only parroting my own thoughts. I don't want a parrot for a wife; I want an individual with her own thoughts and ideals. I want a wife who will bring out the creativeness within me—in thought, deed and aspiration. Barbara ceased to do this. I don't know if the lacking is in me or in her. I *do* know that our relationship became a burden to my mind. Our lovemaking was for her, not me—I derived no pleasure from it. I accepted her love only out of a sense of obligation. Even though I told her time and again that I did not love her, and though she accepted this fact, *I* still felt the guilt of it, and this probably was more detrimental to our relationship than anything else. Still, she clings to me and this clinging is like a millstone around my neck ...

"... Sometimes I wonder why God or I do not let myself love her—and a feeling comes over me that *it is best*, because God has other plans for me—what plans I know not. And there are times when I think I may die soon—that I will not see another spring. I can accept death sooner than I can the idea of making a mockery out of a marriage ..."

I continued to gather dust on my shoes as I plodded the 'lonely road'—alone and groping. That plodding took me away from Pontiac when General Motors asked me to transfer to Dayton, Ohio. I had nothing against Dayton or G.M., but Sealed Power Corp in Muskegon, Michigan asked me to join their Methods Engineering

Group. It promised something different to be learned, so I took the position, and in September 1960 I returned to the shores of Lake Michigan.

The pages of my journal show little mind-activity until this poem I wrote in October 1961 ...

> "I grow weary of life.
> But I have not yet lived.
> I grow weary of ignorance
> But I am not yet wise.
> I grow weary of being weary
> But I have not yet labored.
> I grow weary of longing
> For something to love
> But still I am loved.
>
> I grow weary of life
> for life to me is naught
> but a hollow shell
> full of rattling stones.
>
> I grow weary of ignorance
> For ignorance is the source
> Of all my misery.
>
> I grow weary of being weary
> For the labors of my life
> Have brought me fruits
> That leave me cold and empty.

I grow weary of longing
For something to love,
For my heart is heavy
With tears of crying
Unto the empty night.

There is no life without love
And what worth is wisdom
If love does not light its path.

Labor is bondage
Without love—
And love is but a tear
In my heart.

Life is bondage
Wisdom is a lonely recluse—
And love is but a tear
In my heart."

◆   ◆   ◆

Muskegon offered a change of scene but little else during my first year there. I belonged to several organizations, started another ski club, but judging from my 12 December 1961 journal I was still alone when I wrote …

"Somewhere in this terrifying farce we call a world, there must be a reality. Casting aside the hypocrisy of religion, the ignorance and incompetence of government—beyond the blind stupidity and apathy of the masses—with its ridiculous standards of morality and moronic sense of values—its expert excuses for ignoramic action …"

I stopped writing at that point, must have paused for a time, then continued ...

"There must be a reality, for with all the non-reality—this tragic comedy I see in the world—there must be a contrast, or how else could I perceive the fallacy in what I see?

"If all that I perceive *without* is non-reality, then that contrast—that Reality that gives perception—must be *within*.

"If non-reality pervades the universe, then so must reality—for contrast—and if reality is that 'constant' *within* me, then That which is *within* also pervades the universe, and if That pervades the universe, then TAT TWAM ASI." (That Thou Art.}

The above was written just as it flowed from my mind—an engineer's mind—and it was clear to me what *I* meant when I wrote it, but remember, the scribbling on those pages was never meant to be understood by another mind.

I may not have had a kindred spirit in those days, but often I would come home after work, make myself a Manhattan, sit down on the couch of my trailer home and *think;* I'd let my mind fly into realms it chose to explore. At those times I would be in an ecstasy of pure thought and concentration, free of distraction or obligations outside of my own mind. There have been times since then that I longed for that mind-freedom ... if only for an hour, a moment ... a nanosecond.

I took several night classes at the local community college in an attempt to pick up some of the Humanities I'd not received in engineering college. One of my classes was 'Philosophy 202—Ethics,' and the professor required a paper to be written and titled, 'My Idea of Ethics.' Below is the paper I wrote in February 1962 and the Professor asked me to read it before the class ... He obviously liked it.

"My idea of ethics is inseparable with my philosophy of life, however it is not the intent of this paper to expound on every ideal and opinion I may hold. I will instead endeavor to relate briefly the how and why I conduct myself as I do in my relationship with myself and with my fellow man.

"What ever my conduct in life, its course of action is governed to a great extent by my belief in two quotations. First from Confucius, 'The superior man goes through his life without any one preconceived course of action or any taboo. He merely decides for the moment what is the right thing to do.'

"The other I adopted years ago in high school, from Emerson, 'What I must do is all that concerns me, not what others will think.'

"My belief in these two philosophies springs from a deduction I made long ago; that deduction is essentially this:

"This society is made up of millions of people holding almost as many opinions as to what is right and wrong about everything. These opinions are derived from sources ranging from the Bible to the 'Three Stooges,' and lord knows what else. Most ideals and opinions conflict from one person or church to the next, and all consider their own to be correct. It is humanly impossible to satisfy everyone in one's own conduct.

"Every formula or rule of conduct has its origin in some basic truth. Just as in mathematics and physics, the most complicated formula has its beginning in the basic arithmetic of two and two equals four. My solution, 'Find the basic truths and reasons behind all ethics and morals. Having once known clay, I can understand all pottery.

"A person's sense of ethics and morals is no better than his sense of values. I must determine *for myself* what, in *my* brief moment of time—and in time itself—is of true worth. Deduction: 'Only that which is real, everlasting and unchanging can be used to establish a foundation for a life of harmony with oneself and the universe.' The concept of this *Constant Reality* is a subject not to be covered here, but its existence for me, divine or otherwise, constitutes the basis for my sense of ethics and morals. It has no ecclesiastical justification, I inherited it from no one; it is a product of my own search and thought—whatever it is—it is my own.

"One of the greatest faults in most standards of ethics and morals is, people are given 'formulae' into which they inject their situation, turn the crank and out comes their ethical solution. When a situation arises where the conditions do not readily fit into the formula—chaos results. If they knew the basis on which the formula was derived, there would be no problem. I prefer to understand the basis, and have no need of formulae, I '... merely decide for the moment what is the right thing to do.'"

I must add here the comment written by the professor on the bottom of the original paper ...

"Mr. Schrader:
This is an outstanding paper. It is my habit to extract from good papers those phrases, sentences, mainly ideas, which represent a new way of saying something old, or by their content convey something new. In the case of this paper, if you do not keep it, please return it to me. If you decide to keep it, please permit me to have it copied ..."

I also had occasion and cause to write some newspaper comments when the local Prosecuting Attorney began a rampage to censor men's magazines. I wrote this article about censorship, and it was published in the local newspaper in February 1962 ...

"The Prosecuting Attorney has taken upon himself a tremendous responsibility; for not only is he the guardian of our laws and rights, he is now also the sustainer of the 'moral integrity' of our youth. Having taken on this new job, he has done all parents a great service—relieving them of the duty of providing their children with a decent sense of values.

"If the 'moral integrity' of the American youth hangs in balance with the presence or absence of a few magazines in a newsstand, then this nation stands in the shadow of a far greater demon than we now imagine.

"The greatest demon present in this current censorship issue is not pornography or its contamination, but the censorship itself. When one man or one group is given the authority to dictate what the general public cannot read, then the gate is opened onto the road that leads to the dictation of what it *can* read. The histories of totalitarian nations contain the short-sighted people who give a small group the honor of 'protecting' them from 'harmful' literature, then later the same short-sighted people *joyfully* cast their freedom onto the mountains of burning Bibles.

"Whether I choose to read pornography or not, whether Plato or only Pluto, no one, not even the general public, has the right to restrict my right of choice. When even one sentence has been censored from a newsstand or library, my right of choice to read that sentence—whether I would or not—has been taken away.

"What then is the solution to pornography? It is a simple law of economics—no publisher will publish and no newsstand will carry a magazine that is not purchased. So long as there are 'minds' to enjoy pornographic literature, so long will it be published and sold—and not all the efforts of the State or the Church can suppress its growth. If the youth of America prefer to seek this ignorance rather than wisdom, then the failure *and* the solution lies *not* in censorship, but in the home and the individual.

"There can be no solution without a renewal of mind. So long as it is more blessed to hate evil than it is to love beauty, so long will evil be foremost in the mind of Man. So long as the 'forbidden fruits' of a base life are considered more delicious than the 'bread of life,'—enlightenment—so long will Man remain base. So long as the ignorant are called 'hep' and wise called 'square,' so long will Man remain 'hep.' Wise men have taught since the beginning of time that all things—both good and bad—spring from within, and if we would be good, we must have a renewal of self. But then, people like themselves the way they are, so they have 'passed the buck' by having their prosecutors cause these teachers to drink hemlock or to be nailed to a cross. How convenient it all is; now we can have the Prosecuting Attorney be responsible for the failures in our own character."

I attended my first meeting at the local Unitarian Fellowship not long after this article appeared in the Muskegon paper. The discussion at the meeting centered on censorship and the local population's obvious oblivion to its potential problem. I raised my hand and said, "After my letter to the editor appeared in the paper, I received a number of phone calls agreeing with my position." They all looked at me, a stranger in their midst, and asked, 'Who are you?' I told them, 'Bill Schrader.' To my surprise and embarrassment, they all stood and gave me a resounding ovation. They were familiar with my article and were wondering who in the hell I was to write such things with which they all agreed. Without effort, I was welcomed and became an integral part of their group. I learned that one-third of Unitarian groups often consist of engineers and scientists. I wondered what the other two-thirds are, because Ralph Waldo Emerson, Thoreau and many of their contemporary authors were also Unitarians. I went on with this group, to become one of its directors. I would often meet for lunch with other members of the group, sitting around on beer cases in an aisle of Wayne's Deli, munching our sandwiches and discussing 'things worth discussing.' It was even suggested that I become leader of the group—they could call me, 'Rev. Schrader.' We all laughed, but it was an indication that someone had finally listened to what I had to say—and liked what they heard.

◆   ◆   ◆

The end of 1962 left me in a pit of depression, made evident by the scribbles in my journal ...

"Often I have written in here of my despair, but rarely of my joy. One reading this would think I am *never* happy.

"In my despair I need the sanctity of my inner self which seems to find its way into my pen when I write herein. If one is to read of my happiness, then he must also read of my despair, for the same things that lift me to the heights of my heart's song are those that tap the springs of my heart's tears.

"Many are the activities that occupy my hours, but few are there that bring me joy. Before me sits over $1,000 of shortwave radio equipment—the envy of many—I receive no joy from the radio nor from their envy. (I was a ham radio operator.) A mile away sits an airplane which I may fly alone, there is none to share my triumph ... Is defeat less empty? My achievements and my failures balance the scales of my heart, for in neither do I find aught of worth."

And the next entry read:

"And so I enter a new year. So??? Will 1963 be as empty as 1962? How empty was the last year? As I look back to, only three pages in my journal—what took place?

"I met Joan. Our paths crossed briefly and we went our ways—not knowing what one felt for the other. (Joan is the woman to whom I gave warning about being willing to accept 'loneliness' as a companion on the road to Truth.)

"I earned my Private Pilot License.

"I started working with the Port City Playhouse as Stage Manager, and Civic Opera as a stagehand. It is fun and an activity where I have met many people whom I enjoy—some girls—one of whom I dated for a couple months. She fell in love with me, but she did not fill my void. I pass on.

"I am working on a new statue. (When living in Pontiac I had created a clay statue of a woman—some say it was beautiful.) It goes hard. I know what message I want to convey, but the clay in my hands is silent. I want to show a man—the 'Inner Man'—who hangs his head, arms and body in lost despair—bowed by the weight of his ignorance and his world without meaning or purpose or substance—who with complete defeat—or surrender—lifts up his arms and eyes and whispers, 'Oh God, *please* ...'

"Where is the song in my heart? I am a void—neither rapture nor despair do I feel. I have lost the ability to see and feel beauty. Even the ugliness does not fill the emptiness—I am becoming a vegetable—I am living in name only—I no longer feel—I am dead.

"Oh God, pleeease ..."

And more gloom in February 1963 ...

"Reality is a hangover.

"The day is a dark overcast, it snows but not enough to lend beauty to the gloom of the late afternoon. I stand staring sightless out my window, gray with the dirt of winter's smoke stacks; and all is silence—only the whisper of the furnace fan shares my world—occasionally the shout of a child reaches me, echoing out of the distant whiteness—only emphasizing my complete aloneness.

"Suspended thus, my mind's eye turns inward and probes the depths of my misery. A morning of fitful sleep, made worthless and entangled with tormented dreams of a long night of multiplex emotions, has made my misery ripe for the probing eye.

"The words I read long ago now come beating into my troubled mind and engrave their message on the face of my desolation—'A day will come when you shall see your high things no more, and your low things all too near; you shall fear your exaltation as if it were a phantom. In that day you will cry—All is false.'

"And that day cometh. It came like the rains and beat upon the house of my ideals, and the sands of its foundation were washed away. And when the house of my ideals fell, so fell many angels. That which I thought good and true was washed clean and its true nature of ugliness and fallacy was seen. Now I stand amid the debris of my mind and search for any truth with which to rebuild."

There is no indication in my journal or memories to tell me what caused the above depression. Memory tells me this mood was not unique; I experienced many moments of self-doubt and self-hate over the years. Sometimes I would write of them, but most often not; the gargoyle would crouch on my shoulder and glower into my brain for an hour or two, then fly off after feeding on my despair.

April brought my thirty-fourth birthday and with it a brief moment with a woman—in a way I'd never experienced before. She wanted to divorce her husband and marry me. She saw in me the strength she needed in her life and didn't receive from her husband. We tarried, we spoke of love … but I knew that I was only a tool, a-means-to-an-end for her, and after a short time, we went our separate ways. She eventually got her divorce via another 'tool.' Did it matter? I wrote many pages in my journal during this period, but relating them here would serve no purpose, however the last entry in my journal about her summarizes my feeling about the situation …

"Oh, my dearest, can we ever find the happiness we seek if our life together be built upon lies and deceit? You say … the only possible way to obtain your divorce in this society will mean the casting out of all ethics and morals and of truth … And if freedom is purchased at such a price—is the merchandise received there from worthy of the bounty paid?

"If it was our mutual high standards that brought us together, will the compromise of those standards eventually drive us apart? If to hold fast to our ideals means we will never marry ... have we lost more than that which we lose to become married?

"We stand at the threshold and gaze upon the values of our past and our future; of what are we the master and to what do we become slave?

"It is a door though which we must pass, but not without pause, and not without thought, for once having stepped we cannot return."

One item from my journal at this time was about a married couple, with whom I was a friend, and who were on the verge of breaking up ...

"When I was told about Tom and Norma's difficulties, I almost wept. I love them both so much and they have two beautiful children—it just drains my being of the strength to fight. Why do I take their hurt unto myself? Am I trying to absorb their pain thinking it will protect and save them? Perhaps I am merely trying to protect my own illusion of beauty. When there is so much ugliness in the world, why must so many strive so very hard to destroy the beautiful?

"And when I weep, I know not if I weep for my own lost illusions, or if I weep for the world because it cannot see."

◆   ◆   ◆

The end of May 1963 brought into my life a new woman named Elizabeth Houghton. Mutual friends introduced us when Elizabeth was visiting my side of Michigan from her home in Plymouth. We 'hit it off' immediately—danced all night—and the next day I took her flying. She was no stranger to flying, having flown herself in younger years. She told me of her flying escapades and I knew at once, she needed a 'keeper.' We carried on a courtship via letters and many multi-hour telephone calls. We enjoyed many weekends together—in spite of the drive back and forth across Michigan. We explored both sides of the state; we flew to new places and made the most of our few hours out of each week. In November I asked her to marry me and on 18 January 1954, we were married in a simple ceremony at the home of Ed and Grace George in Grand Haven, Michigan.

The last entry in my journal was on 25 June 1963. I didn't stop thinking, but in the early years of marriage there was no time for deliberation over deep thoughts; the task of making a living and home for my wife and her twelve-year-old daughter, Kim, took precedence. Elizabeth harbored less-than-pleasant memories of religion, so I avoided expounding on my philosophies with her, and too, I'd found a *peace* in our togetherness, and my lack of 'journal-weeping' is witness to my new peace of mind.

We moved several times during our first several years of marriage; the low wages I was receiving in Muskegon were fine for a bachelor, but I was now the head of a household and it was necessary to move on. We moved to South Bend, Indiana in the summer of 1966 and spent about a year and a half there while I was employed by the Cummins Engine Co. I found time to write the following attack in a South Bend newspaper ...

"You placed side by side the letters of Rev. Schneiders and Mr. R. R. Rice in this column recently and offered a very interesting contrast. Both used 'science' to support their seemingly opposite opinions. It merely points out that one can find published 'authoritative' proof for *any* argument, provided he is arguing with a person incapable of objective thinking.

"Mr. Rice's sources proved that a high percentage of male delinquents were inspired to crime by movies, but Mr. Rice condemned only the erotic scenes. Why didn't he question the need of the hundreds of violence-oriented teenage-directed movies that are shown in this area every year?

"Mr. Rice did 'prove' that in the case of delinquent girls, twenty-five percent attributed sexual actions directly to an 'erotic' movie. Hurry! Bring on the censor! But wait ... what—to this same twenty-five percent of girls—is considered an erotic movie or picture—or thought? An obscene mind can find obscenity or eroticism in the most pure places ... and of the twenty-five percent, was the movie really necessary to inspire their action?

"Yes, let us all defend our community against immorality, but immorality does not begin and end with sex. Immorality is a product of the human mind, and if a mind is immoral it can taint any or every perception of its own infinitesimal world. And in a world of infinitesimal minds, who is to judge what may or may not offend God—*everyone's* conception of God?"

It was fun rattling my saber, but I never received rebuttals to my various articles in the newspapers—I guess some people just don't have a stomach for battle. That article appeared in 1966 and I never found cause or inspiration to write another.

I managed engineering departments between 1967 and 1993 in Minnesota and became creative in photographic darkrooms. Spending time with the family, usurped my writing in journals. Elizabeth presented me with two daughters; Cyan in 1964 and Pia in 1967 and I found enjoyment in both of them as they grew into adulthood. We played, hiked, skied together and in general, I was the Daddy they remember with fondness to this day, but aside from technical papers, my writing was non-existent. I participated in Unitarian Church groups when distances permitted, and volunteered in the National Ski Patrol for over a dozen years. Our social life was never a large factor in time allocation; we had friends, but we were not immersed in the social merry-go-round. I took up golf at the age of fifty-five, after having inherited a set of clubs, but I used the game more to take a walk with my buddies than to be a proficient golfer—in all the activities of my life I never found a need to be the 'best' at *anything*. I was always my *own* 'yardstick;' 'who I am today compared to who I was yesterday' was all that mattered. I never compared myself to what anyone else did, had or could do; it wasn't important. That attitude was not conducive to my becoming Vice-President of Honeywell, but that, too, was not important. When I retired in 1993, I retired with a smile on my face and moved to Mexico.

6

MEXICO

Mexico, aaahh retirement ... now I'll have time to write that book I've been going to write all my life ... weeelll maybe, after I learn Spanish, then I can start ... weeell, maybe after I travel around Mexico a little ... weeell, maybe after I learn to say, 'NO' to all the volunteer work that is constantly requested of me ... and so it went; retirement life in the Lake Chapala area can be as busy or as un-busy as you want to make it. I would just like to find a happy medium—volunteerism can become a disease. I believe if I'd applied this much time to my job at Honeywell I'd have retired a vice president; now I work my fanny off for no pay.

I started a discussion group in our large expatriate community with the idea of creating a setting where people interested in philosophy, ethics or religion could exchange ideas. It lasted for about a year, but it had evolved into a gathering of people that seemed to want *me* to do all the talking. I didn't want to listen to myself, I wanted their participation—with *their* ideas being created and exchanged. I wanted their enthusiasm to 'kick-start' my stagnant brain into thinking about something besides *things*, but, as groups often do, it too eventually evaporated into the ether of non-participation.

I became engaged in dialogs on an Internet chat room wherein some members needed help dealing with their attempt to *cope*. I responded to their needs in my own way and found receptive minds, and it opened my own need to write again. The chat site created new friendships with e-mail pen pals and I began to exchange ideas with them.

I would like to relate some of the things I wrote to those people who had problems in their lives and were seeking understanding. I responded to their needs in the best way I could, some light or humorous, some a little heavier. Let's see if I have written aught of interest to you, my reader …

Ninnian was the chat room name for one mother whose son asked if Big Bird and Elmo is God. I don't remember what her answer was to her three year old son, but it must have hit a sympathetic cord in my mind when I wrote …

"Thank you, Ninnian. I think you hit the nail on the head. Your 'almost three year old son' is lucky to have a wise mother … even if she is kooky sometimes.

"Too many people seek God through the thousand religions out of fear. God does *not* need our worship or obedience; neither does She need to threaten us with eternal damnation—unless, perhaps your religion needs a God with human faults to relate to, then it's called anthropomorphism (Just being clever here.)

"I was chastised today on this chat site for making an erroneous statement about the Infinite. Being a monotheist, I believe there is nothing in the universe that is *not* God. That's pretty much what monotheism is about. Hence, if there is nothing in the universe but God, then all matter *is* God … and that which is *not* matter, that too is God.

"Consequently, an answer to the question, 'Is Big Bird God?' has to be *yes*, because anyone that says Big Bird is *not* God, is then saying that God *cannot* be Big Bird, and *that* is the finite trying to limit the Infinite … which is rather impossible. Of course, in my monotheistic universe, we are *all* infinite … so it becomes a moot point.

"The whole point is, anyone who says that God is not this or that, is in effect saying … God cannot *be* this or that. And just *who* are we to limit what God can or cannot be?

"Ninnian, your 33 years of experience has done you well. I cannot walk in your moccasins—unless you wear man's size13—but I have walked a few miles of experience in my own. Aren't we *all* here to experience the universe? However large or small we may choose to make it, it is ours to experience. No one can ever understand the God that you see—just be happy that *you* can. Does it really matter if anyone else understands? Oh, it's always nice to communicate with another human being in these thoughts.... but can we ever ... *Really???*"

◆   ◆   ◆

Blob was a person who suggested to the group that all communications are made through some form of energy. I responded ...

"Ah Blob,
"I tried to find my old physics book so I could answer some of your questions ... No luck. You'll just have to put up with my memory—that is both a warning and a qualification....

"Basically ... everything vibrates or has a natural frequency more or less. The spectrum of frequencies range from sub-sound to—well, to be honest with you—they've now come up with names for the *really* high frequencies that I don't recall the names of, but ...

"Sound is defined as those frequencies (vibrations) from 30-30,000 hertz. (cycles in my day)

"*Radio* frequencies used to be about 300,000 cycles to ... geez I don't remember, but UHF is up there in the 300,000,000 cycle range. (I'm open to correction) *Various light* frequencies go on from there.

"There are charts in physics books that can tell you all about it. If you look it up, please share it; you've got my curiosity up now.

"Is there energy in vibrations? Of course ... the whole universe is nothing but one big bucket of energy. Right now, I wish I had a little more of it myself. Chuckle.

"In regards to the solid rock, what makes you think it is solid? If you look close enough you will find that it is buzzing around inside like crazy and *not* solid at all. Ever hear of the space between atoms and the components of atoms?

"That 'rock' can be considered a case of instant cause and effect. The atoms are the *cause* and the rock as we see it is the *effect*.

"You say you haven't come across an energy yet that cannot be put to good use. Wellllll … I have this brother-in-law … (just kidding)

"If, as you say, all things communicate through light, how about ESP and many of the other things we talk about on this chat site?

"You say we listen to sea shells so why not rocks? Okay, but beware, 'communication' is supposed to be a two-way street. Does a rock know it is a rock? Why not ask one? If it answers it may solve a lot of your questions, (but don't tell anyone it answered you).

"I agree, Blob, the pyramids at Giza were built the way they were so that we would ask…. *Why*? Maybe that is their only purpose. But as an engineer, I still ask …'How in the heck …'"

◆　　　◆　　　◆

I responded to Jo and Pam's e-mail with the following:

"Ah ha!! Gotcha thinking didn't I—not that you don't *always* think, but I got *you* wondering about something that *I've* been wondering about too.

"Every cell in this old body of mine has been replaced many times over the years. But if all my physical cells have been replaced, then in what do the memories of childhood remain. To what do those memories cling? That 'essence' to which they cling must not, evidently, be a part of my physical being because all those cells have been replaced many times since childhood.

"I don't think I would call it 'intelligence,' but that 'essence' that made me 'Bill,' when I was still 'Billy,' and was the foundation of the Bill that became me today—Was *that* intelligence?

"Intelligence can be measured—or at least given a number—but that essence that makes me who I am and who you are cannot be measured or quantified. Can it?

"… It has been said, our soul is a part of the only *Soul* and it knows all there is to be known, intelligence is only a human concept.

"It has been said that our soul remembers *everything*; Bill has forgotten but is trying to remember.

"It has been said, once the soul remembers what it *really* is, we will remember that there is *no* past *no* future—only *now*. Time and space is a only human concept.

"The Buddhists are right, *all* is an illusion and our ego perceives the illusion as it chooses. Some perceive misery in their illusion, some joy—it is our choice.

"In the Hindu Gita, it is said, 'Realize that pleasure and pain, gain and loss, victory and defeat are all one and the same.' It is only a matter of perception.

"Ya pays your money and ya takes your choice."

And to Bob I wrote,

"Been there and done that, Bob. Don't have the T-shirt, but I have the memories.

"You can doubt that the Sun will rise tomorrow, you can doubt the year 2000 will come, but you need *never* doubt that God loves you. He loves you whether or not you are a 'good' person, and She loves you without conditions.

"It is a sad thing, that in this world, with millions … nay … *billions* of people out there wanting to be loved … all those lonely individuals crying in the darkness for someone to love them … even many who are married and have families are still crying for someone to love them. There must be a message here.

"I re-read the paragraph I just wrote ... perhaps the message is right there. All these people wanting someone to love *them*, but how many are looking for someone to love? How many conditions do we demand to be met, before we will give our love? Do we say ... *'You love me first, then I'll love you. You drive the right car, have the right job, wear the right jeans* then *I'll love you ... maybe.'* ... Etceteras, etceteras ad nauseum.

"When we desperately *need* to be loved by someone else, we tend to cling too desperately and *demand* to be loved, then that puts too much strain on the relationship—it can never survive.

"When you talk to God, ask Her what to do.... and then *listen.*"

And later, I again wrote to Bob ...

"Touche,' Bob.

"Uff dah! (as we say in Minnesota) I never have figured out women when it comes to the guys they pick. (I never have figured out women as far as that goes, but that's another subject.)

"Back in my 'lonely' years, when it came to women choosing a man, I always figured girls preferred to pick up 'shiny stones' lying around on top of the ground rather than dig a little to find 'real gold.' Can't imagine it has changed a whole lot since then. I don't know in what age range you are, so it is hard to come up with any great wisdom to offer you. I used to kid some of the women during my late single years; I'd say, 'The trouble with women is—by the time they are old enough to appreciate a man with my qualities, they are already married to a clod.' It sounds rather egotistical, but it was interesting how many married women agreed with me.

"You have a curse on you?? Curse smurf! You may have bad breath, but you do *not* have a curse on you—that went out with the Middle-ages (1930 or so). Of course, there was somebody on this website looking to learn witchcraft ... Wasn't a *friend* of yours was it?

"I was at a high school class reunion once when a former female classmate came up to me, put her arm around me and told my wife, 'You know … Bill here was the nicest guy in our whole class.' I turned to her in surprise and charged, 'Why in the heck didn't you tell me that back then? I sure could have used it.

"I suspect, Bob, that you don't smile very often. Believe it or not, there *are* things to smile about *besides* being loved. I didn't smile much either—I had crooked teeth. So I learned to smile with my eyes … darned if people didn't start smiling back.

"This 'love' that you say all the girls are throwing away on 10 to 100 wrong guys. Incredible!! Where do they find the time?? If a girl is *that* flaky, I don't think I'd be interested in her. Maybe you ought to review your priorities, and see just what kind of girl you are trying to catch. We must be careful what we pray for—we might get it.

"Hang in there, Bob."

And more with Bob in a later chat …

"Hello Bob,
'I believe the topic was … what would I need to reach that 'sublime state' of being able to turn off my 'thinker' … Hellsbells, Bob, if I knew that, do you think I'd be here beating on these keys? If I knew that, I'd be in my casita communicating with God. On the other hand … I believe there can be as many answers to that question as there are souls.

"You say there are a lot of people worse off than you … Yes, and there always will be.

"You asked, 'Am I content with my lot?' Relative to what? I want not for my physical needs … Oh, if a genie was to show up beside my computer, I'm sure I could come up with a wish list … If I won the lottery I wouldn't turn it down, but I'm not beating my brains out trying to make my first million bucks … never have, never will; 'tain't my way.

"But do I have longings—do I yearn for ... something ... out there? You bet. *Is it material?* Not really. *Is it physical?* Sometimes. *Is it spiritual?* Has been in the past, but things are pretty *cool* right now. A lot depends on the mood, the emotions, the sun setting over the mountains or the mist coming up from the village. Rather, I have learned to love myself, even though myself isn't perfect. I have learned to love others, even though others are not perfect.

"Would I like something more??? How about something *instead.* Why don't I go after the 'instead??' I could, but I don't know what it is, or if it exists or where to find it. I *do* know this ... when I have searched for that 'instead' across the universe ... I will find it *right here* in my infinite self, where it has *always* been.

"Heaven and hell ... do they exist?? Yes ... No ... Maybe. They are what *we* ourselves make them to be ... no more ... no less. Omar had it pretty good when he wrote ...

> "'I sent my soul through the Invisible,
> Some letter of that After-life to spell.
> And by and by it return'd to me,
> And answer'd "I Myself am Heav'n and Hell.'"

◆   ◆   ◆

I didn't spend all of my waking time on the computer and Internet; I had friends, responsibilities to perform and errands to run in town. I was an officer in a 2500 member local organization and President of another. It became obvious to me that anyone who is willing to volunteer—and fulfill the duties of that position—he'll be welcome to sit on any Board of Directors. I've been a volunteer of one kind or another since high school. I never aspired to *lead* anything—it just always happened. In the Air Force I'd sung in the Base male course, performed in a stage play, instructed an off-duty drill team and took night classes. In college I was president of the photography club, glee club, fencing club and was photography editor of the yearbook and college newspaper. I may have even studied once in awhile. In later years I was active in the Civil Air Patrol and National Ski Patrol. I doubt that I *needed to belong;* I just never learned to say no, and retirement to Mexico didn't teach me to say, "No, gracias."

More from the chat room,

"Bob/Marsha and All,

"OK Marsha, I think you did a pretty good job of it yourself, but maybe I can swing around and hit it from another direction …

"We all have wants and we all have needs, and we all have made the mistake of confusing the two. When we allow our life to be taken over by the illusion of either, we identify with and become possessed by those wants.

"When we identify our self with our illusions it is high time we sit ourselves down and ask, 'Who am I *really*, and who do I *want* to be.' Until we do that and come up with an answer, it doesn't make one bit of difference if that 'right' person comes along or not, because we won't realize it; we are too involved with our own wants and needs.

"How will the 'right' person know you are 'right' for them, if you don't know who you really are yourself? When you have determined who you are, and make your every action an effort toward being that higher person you want to be, you won't be able to hide it from the 'right' person."

A bit of advice to Coy …

"COY

"Reference to your bit about someone detesting the weak …

"I think the word question here is 'detesting' not 'weak.' Who detests the weak, and who cares?

"A person once said to me, 'I hate the _____' I asked, 'How can you hate the _____ when you have never been exposed to them?' He had no answer. Obviously his opinion was worthless.

"I am very strong ... so strong that I can move mountains with my mind ... if I have it in my mind to move mountains. Yet, I cannot think of anyone that I detest. I must admit, I lack a little patience these days with stupidity (ignorance can be fixed, stupid is forever), but there is so much of it running rampant in the world today that I find—to hate or detest stupidity—would occupy too much of my memory bank. So I let it go its own way. Hate is a terrible waste of energy.

"If you *think* you are weak, and you are preoccupied with the illusion that you *are* weak, then you are *de facto weak.* As you think, so shall you be. *You can be no more nor no less than you think you are.* The choice is *yours,* no one else's. What's it going to be?"

Doug had asked the group what the Bible meant when God said, "I am that I am," and I had to give my opinion ...

"Doug,

"I did not tune into the *I am* discussion until lately, but if no one minds, I'd like to put my two-centavo's-worth in also.

"You seem to be in a quandary as to the meaning in Exodus of the "I am that I am" statement. I would like to say first ... if you hope to understand the Bible totally by reading *only* the Bible ... you have a big job ahead of you. I have found by reading the Gita and a few other philosophies I now see the Bible in a different light, and things I didn't understand at the first reading are now seen more clearly. Seeing things in different lights is a wonderful way of seeing the total.

"If I may speak for God in explaining what was meant in the I am statement (and believe me I can only say what *I* think, not what God thinks) ... He/She is saying ... I am *all* that *is* ... and that which is *not* ... that also I am. There is nothing of which you (or anyone) can conceive that *I am not*. I am the *conceiver* and the *conceived* ... I am the *conceiving. I am all that I am* ... there is nothing else.'

"It seems I also heard the word 'truth' being discussed. The 'truth' of Transcendental Calculus is a whole different ball game than the 'truth' of Transcendental Metaphysics. One is provable; the other can only be discussed and argued. If one aspires to Absolute Truth, then that is a totally personal quest and one should not waste time arguing the subject.

"OK, that's my *five* centavo's worth ... we don't have one centavo coins."

◆   ◆   ◆

There was a woman who asked about loneliness ...

"Hi ES,

"Your post this evening got me thinking a bit ... about loneliness of all kinds. If we went back over my journals we would find in my own life many kinds of loneliness.

"In high school ... it was the loneliness of 'too many crushes on the wrong girls' ... who usually never knew or cared (or perhaps never knew but *did* care for me also) ... but never knowing, we moved on to another life.

"Then the loneliness of military life ... no girl friend, no letters, no hopes ... it is loneliness for companionship with the other sex ... and the weariness of too many men. No wonder G.I.s are always horny.

"What about the person who knows the loneliness of seeing too many blank eyes; the thousands of persons you meet on the streets of life that never make eye contact. How can one say hello if the other never makes eye contact? It makes you want to scream … *I am … I have worth … I have something to give!!*

"And then there is the loneliness of the Outsider … the person who sees *too deeply* into life, and is being destroyed by the triviality of it all … and feels he/she is the only person on Earth that sees. Now *there* is *loneliness.*

"The loneliness for family by the person who has none. The loneliness of the fat wishing she was thin, or the thin wishing he was fatter. The loneliness of the wisher … wishing … wishing … wishing … always wishing … and *always* lonely.

"And then there is the person who is lonely to be loved … but what of the person who is loved and is still lonely? Being loved doesn't cure it all. And from the days of crushes, we know that *giving* love does not cure loneliness.

"What then is the cure for the 1001 reasons for loneliness??? Do *we* have anything to say to those lonely voices out there crying in the darkness?? If we do, does that mean *we* are not lonely … or are we …

"And if we are *not* lonely … *why* are we not lonely??"

◆   ◆   ◆

And I wrote of love …

"LOVE AND FEAR

"The two greatest motivations in life are love and fear. The word 'love' gets thrown around every facet of life these days, but it has become more of a 'buzz word' than an expression of true commitment. We love this, we love that, we love each other, but how many of us can truly say we love without conditions? Do we say we love, because it is the thing to say; or are we like the rose that gives forth its scent because its very nature is to *give*—and it is *our* nature to give love. Can we give forth our love, not knowing or caring if it is appreciated or returned?

"Can we love without attachment to the object or fruits of that love? Attachment brings automatic fear, fear of the loss of that object or a person's love. With fear come all the other ills that man is heir to, thus, attachment doth make miseries for us all.

"Can we change the world with love? I doubt it … but we *can* change our *own* little world—that sphere we touch each day with our love of God—because we see God in all persons and in all things.

"Can we say to that person in our mirror each morning, 'I love you first, last and always, because through that person in the mirror I shall know God. Now I can go out and love each and every thing in the universe. Until you can say, 'I love you' to that person in the mirror, you can finger your beads, mumble your prayers, dance to your drums and chant your mantras; but are you getting nothing more than 'warm fuzzies.'

"And for those of you who would deny there is a God … Okay, no judgment, now or later; walk your own path in peace."

More about love …

"LOVE

"OK Craig, as long as all you want are the ideas of others, I will jump in on the band wagon too.

"It is obvious that we all have different ideas about the word *love*. When you say 'chair' you cannot possibly see the chair that is in *my* mind and I cannot possibly see the chair in *your* mind. Seeing the same concept of love is no different.

"'Falling in Love' is a whole different ball game than I 'love' apple pie or whatever. I love my wife and my children, but not the same. When my child accuses, 'You love Mary more than you do me;' I don't try to defend anything. I ask, 'How do you measure that? Do you mean I love Mary two cups more than I do you, or three yards more than you?' How does one measure love? Love is not a *quantity*, it is a *quality,* and quality cannot be measured. I'm not even sure if one can *define* quality.

"The ultimate love is when it is natural. It is *not* something you work at. It is *not* something you get, or expect, or worry about; it is something you *give*.

"If and when one attains the point of knowing God in all things, in all people, and especially in oneself, love will be as natural as the rose that gives its scent naturally and freely—*without conditions*. Can you ever imagine a rose saying, 'I'm not going to smell nice to Joe, he doesn't *appreciate* my fine scent; he doesn't stop and sniff me often enough; he sniffs *other* roses; and he even sniffs that gardeeenia over there' …?' Not likely. That would be comparable to love *with* conditions.

"Can we love the God in all things and persons? Yes. Is that state hard to attain? Heck yes it's hard … But do you have a better option?"

◆   ◆   ◆

I must have written something about the Mayan prophecy that predicts the end of 'this cycle' in the year 2012, because I got a lot of responses and wrote the following:

"Mayas y todos,

"I must have written the magic word; I didn't know so many people were listening.

"Now then, I don't propose to be an expert on the Maya (or anything), but as long as you asked … It appears that most of the cultures of history have in them some common threads weaved in their historical tapestry. Among those threads is a mythology that this Earth has undergone a number of cataclysms, leaving only a few to rebuild/populate/educate the survivors into a new culture; Noah did not have a corner on the myth-market. Many of those mythologies also predict the 'end' in one form or another.

"Sixty-five million years ago an asteroid did a pretty good number on the dinosaurs, and a good thing too, or we'd all be *wearing* scales not stepping on them. Science tells us that when (not if) another asteroid hits the Earth, it will wipe out life as we know it. Is an asteroid going to hit just before Christmas 2012? I'd like to be around then, just to see if the Mayans were right.

"If the cataclysm—in what ever form—does come and wipe us all out, that would really fulfill Nostradamus wouldn't it. You want peace? No *people* on the planet makes for a lot of peace ... I wonder what will take over the Earth then? The insects? How long will *they* keep the peace? What Gods will *they* worship? Will they make their God in their own image too? Will they slaughter each other over their religious convictions? I can see it all now ... '*My God is the only TRUE God, he has three antennae and is green. YOUR God has only two antennae and is brown, therefore I must kill you and ten million others like you. You better worship my God or I'll get my can of RAID and kill you all ... so you'd better bow down or bow out.*"

◆   ◆   ◆

Somebody on the site brought up the idea of a perfect world, so I had to rise to the bait ...

"What is a 'perfect world?'
"Well, if you believe Dr. Pangloss, (of Candide fame) we're *living* in it. Obviously what is perfect for the good doctor ain't necessarily perfect for everyone else.
"Someone wrote in here, Peace, Understanding, No change ... *No change?* The universe and life is in *constant* change; we could not exist without it.

"Peace? Hummmmm, what is that? Guess that means 'World Peace.' Does it matter if the world is at peace if our mind is in conflict?

"Understanding? I assume that means a two-way street. Is that a 'you understand me—I understand you' kind of world? Is that total understanding or just enough to get by? Do you *really* want me to understand you completely, or would you like to retain a little mystery? I'm not sure if I want you to understand the workings of *my* mind, especially when I'm not sure I understand it myself.

"It seems to me that we can get along okay with our material world if we can just get along with one another ... But, on the other hand ... 'I *really do* want that new Lexus, and I should get the kids that new RV; and the house at the lake could use an addition for parties. Let's just hold off on that 'perfect world' until I get a few more of my material *needs.*'

"Somebody once said something about a 'a renewal of mind;' I wonder if that might have something to do with a 'Perfect World?'"

◆   ◆   ◆

One evening I was on-line with the chat room when I smelled rain; there is no sweeter aroma than the first rain after the long dusty dry season. I quickly dashed off this ...

"RAIN??

It is the dry hot season where I live.
The fields and mountainsides are dry and brown.
There has been no rain for eight or nine months
There is no drought, it is just the way things are.

The wind tonight is restless
The trees wave their arms wildly and then are still

The wind-chime sings its song to the darkness and then is
    silent

The night is confused and unsure of itself

What is that I hear? A plane? Thunder?

It can't be thunder, there is no rain … not for another
    month.

But there are no stars … no Mars to my east … there must
    be clouds … but …

That smell; that sweet wonderful smell … can it be??"

◆   ◆   ◆

One person was so miserable he/she called himself,'Sad'. I sent my
sage advice …

"Hola SAD,

"You asked a very good question when you asked. 'What does it
really mean to love myself?'

"A lot of learned people throw that bit around about 'love yourself
first' (I do it myself) but what *does* it really mean? Who can give you a
formula in ten words or less to make it happen? Not I. Even those of us
who are loved by many cannot always feel we are truly deserving of that
love. We think we are not *worthy* … We think, *How can this wretched
soul be worthy of anyone's love? Why* shouldn't *people walk all over me …
I* deserve *it …*

"And so it becomes a self-fulfilling prophecy. We gets what we
expects. Sometimes we even unconsciously encourage people to walk
all over us or take advantage of us, just so we can say, *Seee, I told ya,
men are no damned good!! (or women as the case may be)*

"You have the sound of desperation about you, SAD. When one is desperate one tends to hold too tightly to the object of that desperation. The desperation can quickly turn to fear of loss and that *fear* can cause the destruction of the tenuous bonds that may be holding things together. Do not wear SAD around your neck, it could stand for 'Single And Desperate.'

"One of the troubles with seeking out the 'physically beautiful people'(as you put it) is that you walk right by the *truly* beautiful people. One needs a *self-definition* of what beauty is, not what the TV commercials tell us to believe. Men are often criticized for being more interested in a woman for her looks than her brains; how many women have cared to looked at *me* and wonder what my IQ. might be?

"So you are not *comfortable* being single. Is that because you don't like being alone or do you fear it is a sign of being unworthy??

"Use your time alone to think about something besides yourself and how sad you are. The day will come when you will cherish your alone time and you will cry, 'I have no time for myself.'

"If you have a God, then know that your God loves you without conditions. He loves you no matter how you see yourself or how others think they see you. God only wants for you what you want for yourself and to be happy ... and to remember. You are only in this life for a brief moment, so don't let the small stuff wear you down ... and it's *all* small stuff.

"First thing you must do is change the name SAD. There is a 'gee-whiz' weapon in the Army called SADARM ... it means Seek And Destroy Armor. You are not seeking to destroy, but you *are* identifying with the sadness that it infers. Be happy ... from within."

I wrote a short story that fits with the above note to SAD ... it was published in a local magazine ...

THE PLATFORM

"The wind, armed with icy teeth off Lake Michigan, chased a paper cup down the train platform past peeling green benches and dropped it at the foot of a rusting steel column. The wind paused, and with a devilish grin, shook a red coat and caused the woman inside to crouch and wrap her arms around her calves. She pressed her head and its red knit cap to her knees, her eyes closed and faced away from the bitter blast.

The wind moved on and swirled its thin dirty snow across the tracks, up the brown bricks of an apartment building to rattle a soot-grimed window. Inside, a sleeved forearm wiped away the fog that was created by hot breath against cold glass.

It was 5:14 PM and every day, Monday through Friday, that window witnessed the same forehead pressed against its pane. Willis would remain at the window long after the 5:20 commuter had clattered out of the station, and its dingy green cars disappeared beyond its slowly settling cloud of dust and debris.

The fading winter light found its disinterested way though a cracked window and into his shabby one-room apartment. The spattering of one frying pork chop broke the silence, and the smell of its hot grease joined the accumulated odors of a thousand other meals cooked amid that confined clutter.

In August he had started observing the young woman in red wait for her train; when a summer tan had clothed her arms in gold, and light dresses clung to her slender body. His affection continued to follow her each evening, when she wore sweaters the color of autumn leaves and the breeze played in her long, blond hair. When a blue raincoat protected her from the November rain, she shivered in the shelter of that same steel column, and he cloaked her in his empathy. December snows brought bright roses to her cheeks, and he longed to help as she juggled Christmas packages, and he wondered … 'For whom?'

When January winds drifted dirty snow beside the crumbling concrete, he watched and wondered … *Who is she? What does she do? Is she a student? A secretary? A waitress? Perhaps she is a princess—escaping her lonely protocol prison—I know she is lonely; loneliness etches lines on one's demeanor—lines that only the lonely can read.*

It didn't matter to him who she was or what she did, he knew *she is lovely and gentle; she is life and laughter, and she is all he'd dreamed a perfect girl would be.* Each night he dreamed a perfect world around her and the life they'd have together—after he executes his plan. But … in the tiny world of his aloneness, time expands and contracts and spins without definition—and his resolve changes frequently as the months move by—but now he plans …

"I will wear my best suit, with just the right tie and shirt—nothing too loud—she must know I'm concerned about my appearance, but not preoccupied with it. I must wear a confident countenance without appearing smug. I must be worldly, but embrace those who are not. I must be gentle without being weak. I must be …" but doubt darkened his world, and he wondered …

What MUST I be? What does SHE want in a man? Does she want the men on television who fascinate girls? No, I cannot be one of them … Why do women crave THEM as their dream men … They are vain and shallow, without a grain of passion or compassion … They are all the things I've spent my life trying NOT to be—I've always striven to be myself—to be an individual without embracing individualism; but … I've never been able to resolve the perpetual plight of the individual—loneliness. She too has known the sadness of being unseen—not the pain of rejection—but the sadness of never knowing eye contact with another caring human. And her sadness—like mine—isn't for herself, it is for those who will never know life, because they have eyes to see, but do not see.

His plan is firm and he is prepared; with the *right clothes*—cleaned with hope and pressed in anticipation—hanging in the closet; the *right* shoes are polished and waiting. *Soon, very soon I will meet her*, he'd vowed again and again and again—but always—the *perfect* time was that glow on the horizon of tomorrow …

Spring rains brought new hope. The winds, from beyond the sprawling city's concrete, gathered the fragrance of new life and whispered gently through his open window. *"Now,* now is the time. Today is the day; it is spring, it is warm, this is the *perfect* day."

He sang his hope aloud, "Now I'll dress in my suit and walk down the platform toward her; I'll pause, look up and down the track, and pretending confusion, I'll ask if this is where I should stand for the 'number nine.' I will strike-up a conversation, and 'learn' her stop will just happen to be the same as mine.

"When we part, I'll tell her I will look forward to seeing her again tomorrow. It may take many trips together, but in time we will have a dinner date, then more dates, and then someday ... I can only hope."

He dressed carefully, dusted his black shoes, combed his hair again, put just the right amount of cologne on his cheeks, and brushed his suit one more time. He paused at the door and checked off his plan. He had the *right* clothes, the *right* haircut, the *right* time. His plan was perfect and he'd rehearsed it a dozen times.

He closed the door behind him, and walked confidently down the hall—the tip of his *white* cane preceded him with its tap, tap, tap, tap."

Many people commented on this story, but most missed the fact that Willis is *blind* ...

◆   ◆   ◆

Bob came back, still searching for his dream-mate and I answered him ...

"Well Bob, now that we have totally saturated you with our wisdom and philosophies, you must be totally satisfied and happy. Right? ... *No??*

"I guess philosophies don't do much to warm your feet on a cold winter's night, nor do they share a beautiful sunset or a Brahms concerto. On the other hand, 'dream-mates' might have ice cold feet or prefer to watch a sitcom rather than a sunset, or listen to rap rather than a rhapsody. Neither male or female dream mates come with guarantees.

"We all said you should first love yourself because God loves you, but that idea doesn't quite replace the idea of a nicely scented head resting on your shoulder, does it.

"Now that we have all proven to you what a great guy you are, it is time to go out there and prove it to everyone else—not just the girls. (We're convinced they wouldn't recognize it anyway, and being *great* just doesn't compete with 'exciting, crazy and wild.')

"Marsha had a number of great thoughts when she wrote, "Don't look too 'needy.'" She is right, desperation doth make fools of us all. Yes, decide what kind of girl you want, *but* don't demand attributes she can never have. No one can ever live up to that perfect mate we create in our own minds. And when we say we just want someone we can talk to, remember, that *someone* might just have something worthwhile to say also. So learn to listen. Listening is a good idea anyway; it makes the other person think you are really *intelligent*.

"Try volunteering for something. You don't have to go out and save the world, but ... Amateur Theater is great place to meet people. I found it to be a great way to meet a large cross-section of the population. You don't have to act; there are all kinds of things to do around the theater. Become involved with something beside your own emotions. I have found if you show that you are willing to do a little work for nothing, you will have to fight people off with a stick.

"So, Bob, put a smile on your face—and in your eyes—get your heart off your sleeve and get involved with something in the world besides *Bob*. Keep us informed, we are pulling for you."

◆   ◆   ◆

There were many other times when I exercised my thinking and writing skills on that website; some of the people contacted me directly with e-mails and we had conversations. Some are still friends and we communicate, only one have met face to face. One of my short-time e-mail pen pals received this note from me …

"Hi Colleen,

"You live in South Africa, how about that. I didn't even detect the accent in your letter. Chuckle.

"Well, I'm glad that South Africa is concerned about the environment. Mexico needs an awakening in that regard. They are trying, (?) but politics, politics, politics, plus a certain wandering astray of funds makes the environment part of mañana. (To us gringos that means, 'Not necessarily tomorrow, just not today.')

"Finding a 'soul mate' is one tough job. I was single for eight years after college. Did I marry my soul mate? Perhaps. Have I ever met a potential one since then? No.

"It might be interesting for us to discuss *our* definition of soul mate. Actually, the term is somewhat new to me, having run into it recently on the chat room. When it comes to soul mates, I guess one of the first things to ask of your self—and a potential soul mate is … 'What is important to me and thee?' Also, I guess … 'Why do we *want* a soul mate? If it is just to get married to someone with whom to chase the great 'American Dream' … there ain't no such thing; it is a false dream of materialism and empty promises.

"What is important to me and thee??? (I never have tried to define this idea before, so we are embarking upon a new adventure together.) I am a thinker … a dreamer … a wanna-be writer … a romantic … a philosopher … a lover of Eastern philosophy (in its original, not its New Age variations). Mix all that up with the fact that I am also an engineer … with all that engineering logic to confuse the issue. I am not a Christian in the popular sense of the word. I do not believe in organized religions; they have caused more problems in the history than they have solved. If someone else wants religion, fine—just don't try to push his ideas on me. Do I believe in God? Yes, but *my* God says,

'By *whatever* path you come to me I shall welcome you, for all paths are mine.'

"Why do we want a soul mate? I have been heard to say ...'The greatest happiness is to share *something* you love with *someone* you love.' Does that mean thee has to give up the things thee loves and love only mine? Of course not, but it does mean ... Don't fake loving the same things *I* do as a means of getting from me what you want.

"What is expected of a girlfriend? I cannot speak for anyone but myself, and I know what I want is different than what seems to be the popular trend. Let me ask you, What is expected of *boyfriends?* I didn't know the answer to that question when I was in high school, and my knowledge hasn't improved any. It always seemed to me that girls are looking around for gold laying on top of the ground. (Of course where you are maybe that happens) That means, they expect all the great and sparkling things about a man to be just hanging out there for them to pick. But they'll pass blindly by those hidden gold mines rather than dig a little. If you think I am sounding bitter, no—I'm just remembering how I used to feel about the subject.

"I use to 'toss out a bait' and see if any girl would rise to it. What I mean is, at some time early in a relationship I'd drop a bit of Gibran or some other pearl of wisdom very quietly. If the girl got a twinkle of recognition in her eye, I'd explore further. If no twinkle ... then no interest. I'm afraid there are an awful lot of eyes out there that don't twinkle. Do your eyes twinkle, Colleen?

"Well, right now the stars are twinkling in Mexico and I've mumbled on long enough.

"Hope I haven't bored you too much, falling asleep at your desk at work is a no no.

"Tu amigo, Bill"

◆   ◆   ◆

David and I communicated for a brief time; his questions are preceded by > which helps to know what's going on …

"Hola David,
"I'm glad you liked my last email; I'll have to go back and see what I said. You know, on the chat room, I don't always like to see those words, 'smile,' 'grin,' 'heheheh,' etc., but I've found that on email you can't always know when a person is just kidding. In my ham radio days we used to say, 'Hi.' That means, 'I'm just joking—don't take me seriously.' So, if it is ok with you, hereafter I will use 'Hi' when you aren't supposed to take me dead serious.

David wrote:
>I am so hungry for souls that have a deep passion to find and discover
>what the purpose of life is all about. So many seem de-sensitized to this, and
>when the subject is brought up to them, they really don't care; as if life's
>material aspects are more than enough to fulfill their souls. And I've felt
>so alone in this respect for soooooooooo long.

"You remind me of my younger days. I sought a girl for my own, hoping to find one who could see as deeply into life and beauty as I did. I found a lot of girls, but found none that *really* understood. They were 'good Christians' and although they might have talked a good game about the things I loved, it usually turned out all they wanted me for was my body … hi/2 (That's only a half a hi, I'm not totally kidding.) I was probably, economically, a good 'catch,' but I thought I had more to offer than the income from a good job.

"I once told a cute young thing whom I met in a post grad class, 'If you choose to walk the path to Truth, be prepared to be lonely ... for few there will be you will meet along that path.' I might have found companionship with her, but she was ten years younger than I ... and our paths just seemed to part after school was out.

>I actually began to cry at how beautiful your response was/is and how
>awesome you must be!

"Well thank you; I didn't think I had written anything *that* profound. I do write things once in awhile that make tears come to *my* eyes, but that's probably more from the joy of writing than for the content.

>I love you Bill; is that wrong? Does it make you feel odd that I
>said that I love you? Is it O.K. to be this open about our feelings for one
>another especially from one man to another?

"You will find in CONVERSATIONS WITH GOD the teaching that, once you realize God is in *all* and you love God, then you too will love *all*. Too many people can think only in terms of romantic love and all it represents (good and bad). I advocate 'love without conditions.' When we can love all of God's creation *without conditions* then we can find happiness in loving—whether we get loved back or not.

"How many times have we seen/heard the situation that says ...'I'll love you ... *if* ... or *but?*' I like to use a perfect example of love without conditions ... My dog Scooter loves me twenty-four hours a day, seven days a week, whether I feed him on time, fuss over him, take him with me or leave him home; he tells me in his own way ... I love you

Daddy. I love him in the same way. If he gets me up six times during the night to go pee, I love him and don't mind my loss of sleep. If he tangles with a skunk and I have to deal with that for weeks, I still love him, and feel sorry that he has to put up with himself and his own smell. He doesn't expect anything out of me and I don't expect anything out of him. I have never had to discipline him because he has never in nine years required disciplining. And everybody in town loves Scooter; when I show up at the coffee shop in the morning (there are about 6 of us gringos that tend to drink our coffee and read USA Today together in the morning) they all say 'hi' to Scooter and pet him and are glad to see him; they *might* say good morning to me. I went into a small mall … three different shop owners asked where Scooter was (I'd left him in the car). I don't think they even know *my* name. Scooter is a Lasha Apso. He is my friend, not my dog. One woman who saw us at the coffee shop this morning—whom I don't recall seeing there before—said to me, 'That dog sure loves his Daddy.' I said, 'Yup, and his Daddy sure loves him.' Well, I'm sure you didn't want to hear about my pooch, but I just wanted to get across the idea of unconditional love. If two people could love each other the way Scooter and I do, their life would be great.

>How old are you?

"I have refrained from telling my pen-pals my age. Not that I have any hang-ups about age, it is that I'd just as soon let people retain their own mind-picture about my physical being—even though I *do* look like Cary Grant (Hi).

>I think that's so fucking awesome that you're living in
>Mexico. Or isn't it. Are you their by choice or are you avoiding something?
>Is your wife like-minded? What made you want to go to Mexico?

"We love Mexico and the Mexican people. The weather is near perfect, the cost of living is better than the States and we have a lot of friends here now. We are very busy and healthy—and no—the FBI or IRS is not looking for me; at least I don't think so. Hi!

>I'm originally from Chicago, where a very large Latino community exists.
>I'm considering going back there for good.
>I am not happy here in Florida.
>I would also absolutely love to live and experience the Western United States.
>I've been to Colorado once and immediately fell in love.

"I can understand that too. Been there, done that and flown over them many times. If we didn't live here we would probably live in New Mexico.

>Ever since I can remember I've had a very deep attraction to Mountains and
>the Ocean and all of nature. I feel that out West I'd be happiest, like the
>vibration of the land there best compliments my soul, ya know. Have you
>ever felt that way about a place you've been too?

"I once drove from Albany, OR to Calistoga, CA when I was out there on business. As I drove past Ashland, OR something just 'pulled' me into the town. I had a very strong 'feeling' about that town, as though I wanted to return. We even considered the area for retirement someday. It won't happen that way, but it is one of the few places that ever *attracted* me. I once spent several weeks at an Air Force radar site out on the tip of Montuak Point, L.I., NY. That place really drew me to it also. There was no way to make a living, but if you love looking at the ocean that's a great place to do it.

>To me life is about experience, and how one chooses to be in relation to
>how those experiences may or may not affect the one's soul and consciousness.

"Life's experiences is what it's all about. We are here so that God can experience Herself though us. We have no other purpose. If we choose to be 'good or bad' it doesn't matter; He does not judge us. He does not send us to eternal damnation—that idea was invented by priests-types for job security—our soul is perfect, always has been and will ever be; there is nothing we can do here in this life to change that. One might ask, 'Why I am I trying to be good? Why can't I go around doing bad things and have a lot of fun like the 'other' people?' Well, if doing 'bad' things is what you think you want to do and be, go right ahead. If that is the highest person you want to be, go ahead on—*but think hard*

"I was flying back from Seattle in April at about 30,000 feet over the Rockies. I got to thinking about some things my daughter and I had talked about in the way of listening to God. I kinda composed a dialog that would go something like … 'Well, Pia, why don't you turn off the TV, put the dogs out and set yourself down to quietly *think*; then just ask God a question … something simple like … *God, what is the meaning of life?*' Then listen. Then *I* got to thinking …'Yeah God, what *is* the meaning of life.' Darned if He didn't come right back with the answer right there in that DC-9 at 30,000 feet. God told *me* the meaning of life—and I didn't even have to climb a mountain in the Himalayas to talk with a Guru. Do you know what He said?? … I'm not going to tell you. I'm going to let *you* ask God yourself and then you can tell me. I'll let you know if She is consistent with His answers. (You notice

I keep switching genders on God. What ever gave Christians the idea that God needs a gender?)

>I hope I haven't freaked you out. I mean no dis-respect.

"I can't remember ever having been 'freaked-out.' I can't even think what *could* 'freak-me-out.'

> Do you cus? For whatever it's worth, sorry if I offended you.

"Do I cuss? Only at myself—and an occasional other driver. I used to cuss like all good soldiers do, but then I looked around and saw who else was cussing. I figured cussing put me in the same category as they. I stopped. I don't mean to imply that I think I'm better than they are; I just want my language to indicate who *I* am. I don't cuss, for the same reason I try to speak and write proper English. I *try* to use correct grammar, spelling, capitalize where one should and all those things, just because it is the *correct* way of doing what I am doing. I cannot earn a living as an engineer doing things correctly and then do things incorrectly after I leave the office. To do that would (1) not be *me,* and (2) would be rather juvenile. I ain't going to do either. (I must say though, thank God for Spell Check on my computer; I'm a lousy speller.)

"Tell me what you've read, David, to get where you are in your thinking. Tell me what you think.

"And it is time for me to start thinking about preparing dinner; I do the cooking in this house and my wife does the baking. Works out fine, I like to cook—she doesn't. She likes my cooking and never complains. She does the laundry, I do other 'stuff.' Sooooo, I'd better get crack'n,' besides, the thunder is on the mountain again.

"Over to you,

"Bill"

◆   ◆   ◆

Sidney was an adolescent with familiar adolescent problems …

"Hola Sydney,

"There is nothing wrong with preferring a quiet walk with the dogs as opposed to the babble of the crowd. *There is much to be heard in silence.*

"Your walking down the school hall hugging the wall isn't all bad, at least it keeps you out of the way of those running down the middle.

I used to be very quiet too—still am really—fooled a lot of people that way; they thought I was super intelligent. What is the old saying? 'Better to remain quiet and let people think you are stupid than to open your mouth and confirm it.'—present company excepted of course.

"You speak of being a loner. It depends on what path you are walking. If you choose to walk the *Path*, then you must prepare yourself to be lonely, because few there be whom you will meet along that Path.

"Enough already, Bill"

◆   ◆   ◆

My files and memory give no indication that anyone ever took my 'sage advice;' actually, not many of my pen-pals gave indications they took *any* of my advice. Perhaps it was because I didn't tend to *give advice*—it was 'food for thought' … I tried to make them *think.* People are much more receptive to a solution if they come up with themselves. I like to plant the 'seed,' and then let the reader tend the garden and harvest what *they* have discovered about life—and about themselves. That's how I used to work in the engineering world; I'm not sure how it works in the world of philosophy.

Confucius said, "I won't teach a man who is not anxious to learn, and will not explain to one who is not trying to make things clear to himself. And if I explain one-fourth and the man doesn't go back and reflect and think out the implications in the remaining three-fourths for himself, I won't bother to teach him again."

I don't purport to be a teacher on the level of Confucius—but I do like to throw seeds around. I try to speak my truths softly and clearly, if there are ears to hear, let them hear.

One evening in the summer of 1999, while washing dishes for my lovely wife, I told myself, 'I'm going to write a book, it will be a love story ... kind of a BRIDGES OF MADISON COUNTY for men. The woman of that novel was stuck in a life that had not filled her dreams, had never met her soul mate. Why can't a man have dreams too?

7

THE BOOK

During the summer of 1999 I spent many hours on the Internet, writing to people I didn't know but who listened to what I had to say. Whether they really listened, understood or used anything I'd said I never knew, but in an effort to help them, I had to *think*, and the exaltation of thinking and writing kindled a new flame in my brain and I began to write—something I'd wanted to do all my adult life—to create a book that Mr. Krause dreamed I would someday write. I wish he were alive today and could witness what he quietly inspired so many years ago.

I didn't just sit down at my computer one day and decide to write a book, the idea evolved from a poem I'd written extemporaneously one evening and then e-mailed to my pen pal, a university professor in Canada. I decided the poem was incomplete and immediately wrote the second half and sent it to her. She said it brought tears to her eyes; she wanted to have it read over a local radio station.

I liked the idea of her shedding tears over my poem, so I wrote a short story around the poem and sent it to her. She wanted to send it to a magazine for publishing—and if I didn't, she would.

I started the novel and intended to use the short story as the first chapter. I told my pen pal about my idea and she wrote back, "Oh, I knew you were going to write a book when you sent me the second page of the poem; it is just too powerful to remain only a poem." That was encouragement—now all I needed was something to say.

The love story's locale is Mexico, and the main character is a fifty year old man who falls in love with a young Mexican woman. The

story, however, evolved with dialogs carrying 'deeper thoughts.' I
hadn't started out to write a philosophy, but philosophical words
flowed from within as I remembered things I'd forgotten for a million
years. I hoped I could get the reader involved with the story and then
slip them words of wisdom when they weren't looking—perchance to
make them think. I was now writing to people who don't read 'deep'
books.

I have read many books of 'deeper thoughts,' but have found many
authors become enraptured with their own verbosity and grand vocabulary, to the end they lose their reader, and in the end their weighty
thoughts have been written to themselves. In my book I choose to
communicate to my reader by using the character of a young Mexicana
who is searching for answers in life. Her limited grasp of English allows
me to use simple dialog, and present my message in terms that the
character—and any reader—can understand.

I would like to share with you the poem that evolved into that first
novel ...

"TELL ME
by
William J. Schrader

I cannot tell you I am 'in-love' with you;
For the *you* in my heart is only *my* dreaming.
You may be greater than my dreams,
But I know not truly the person I love.

And tell me not that you are 'in love' with me;
For you do not know me.
You can be *in love* with your imaginings only.
Come—let us learn of each other together.

Come—sit with me—and tell me of your dreams.
Tell me what lifts you to the heights of your joy.

Tell me what drives you to the depths of your despair.
Tell me what brings songs to your lips and tears to your eyes.

Tell me who you *are and* who you wish to be.
Tell me *who* you are, but not *what* you are.
Tell me *who* you wish to be, but not *what* you wish to be.
Tell me *where you are* along your path.

Tell me where your path is leading, not that it has stones;
Life's stones can be diamonds, but life's path must have a dream.
Tell me if you walk alone or do you need companions;
Some may share your walking, but none can fully share your longings.

Tell me of your dreams, but dream not that they are my dreams;
For your dreams are seen though your eyes, and mine are mine alone.
Tell me your dreams are pearls, but string them not for me.
For your pearls can become stones around *my* neck.

Tell me we can dream together, but not the same dream.
For dreams, however close, are never the same.
Tell me we can live together, but not the same life.
For two lives cannot be lived as one.

Two lives cannot be lived as one, but
Let us fold our lives together,
For the strings of the harp, though separate, fold their music into one,
And our heartstrings may learn the joy of life's song together.

Let me tell you *my* dreams, that we might dream together;
For dreams, though not the same, can *share* the hearts of two.
Share with me our two dreams, that we might know their joy together;
For dreams shared with a *beloved* are the greatest joys of life.

Tell me you must give love and be loved in return.
I tell you, love must be given without conditions.

Tell me that you love me, but *not* that you need me or want me;
For I can fill your love, but not fully your needs or your wants.

Tell me that you want to know the depths of *my* being,
That you may love the person I am and not the person you imagine.
For the person I am may transcend the peaks and the valleys
of your imagination.

And ... tell me ...
Do you hold the wonder of the stars in your fingertips,
That your touch can lift me to the heavens?
And can you leave your being on the wind,
That the essence of your embrace remains—softly in the curve of my
arms?

Tell me that you love me fully, but not forever;
For ever is in the hands of Forever and we have but a moment.
Forever may be too short to hold our love,
But we can hold Forever in our love.

Come, tell me what brings songs to your lips and tears to your eyes;
That I may understand.
Tell me what path you walk and where it leads;
That we may share our paths, in these *our* moments of Forever."

This poem has been translated into Spanish and has found its way into many homes. Mexican men and women love it and hang it on their walls. To my surprise, it caused many tears to flow, and inspired the name of the novel, KISS MY TEARS AWAY.

The main male character, John, has occasion to express his thoughts and give answers to some of life's deepest questions. His words are my philosophy of 'life, death and whatever.' The words are not spoken to convince anyone to my way of thinking, but only to suggest there are other ways to think about questions that have for too long been given empty answers by 'learned men' who say, 'God works in mysterious ways and we are not meant to understand everything.' I say to those learned men, I already understand everything—I have merely forgotten. I am now trying to remember that which I have always known—or the essence that inhabits my body has always known. What is that essence? John explains it to Laurina in the novel ... Laurina is John's masseuse, with whom he has fallen in love.

They pause mid-way through his massage and sit together on her massage table as he reads a letter he has written to her ...

"Mi Laurina,

"You asked me to tell you about souls. You ask good questions—hard to answer—but questions that make people think are always good questions. I can only answer about souls from what I know in my heart.

When I read this to you please stop me and ask questions, I want you to understand all that I say to you.

First, mi amada, know that so long as we are in human form, we can never fully understand about souls. Our souls are a part of the One Soul, and this is another way of saying, 'God.'

She touched his hand, "Does this mean, after we are no longer in human form—after we die—then we will understand all about souls?"

He laid the paper aside, "Yes, but actually, we know and understand right now, we have merely forgotten. We are here in this life to remember—to remember who we truly are, here inside." and he placed her hand on his chest. There was a lack of understanding in her eyes, so he smiled, kissed her on the forehead and said, "Be patient, you shall understand in time."

He continued, "One problem with understanding about souls is—our Christian teachers have taught us there is a God, a Jesus, a Holy Spirit, a Mary, a Devil, a heaven and a hell—all kinds of conflicting deities and journeys that confuse us when we try to think." She nodded her head in agreement.

He paused, noting her concentration, then continued, "Because of the way we are taught to believe, we think there are many things out there warring for our souls, our attentions and our sacrifices. We are told that we are here only by the grace of God; and to scare us into believing this, we are taught we must do *exactly* the right things, or we will go to hell for all eternity—with purgatory thrown in for good measure in the case of you Catholics." He smiled at her.

She pulled back, "Do we not *all* have to suffer purgatory?"

"As far as I know, yours is the only major religion that has that condition."

"That is not fair." Then grinning she asked, "If I become a Protestant, can I skip purgatory and go right to heaven?"

"You, my angel, will go straight to heaven in any case." And he kissed her on the tip of the nose.

He paused and pulled the blanket up on his shoulders again. She tucked it around his bare waist, "Are you cold?"

"A little."

She moved closer against him and put her arm around his waist under the blanket, touched his bare skin with her cool hands and made him jump. She giggled an apology, hugged him closer, and rested her head on his shoulder. It remained there for a few moments, then she raised her cheek to his, "If you do not believe in purgatory, do you believe in heaven and hell?"

"Yes, right now I'm in heaven, and when we are apart, I am in hell." She leaned back and scowled at him, but he laughed and pulled her back, saying, "I couldn't resist that, but I will tell you."

She relaxed against him as he continued, "Do I believe in a heaven where we will have all the riches we didn't have in this life; where we spend every day with our dearly departed loved ones and sit around on clouds playing harps and listening to choirs of angels all day? No. Do I believe in a hell where we suffer the torment of fire and brimstone for eternity, because of some sin we committed in our one-chance lifetime?

No—if for no other reason than there is no hell, never has been, never could be."

She frowned and asked, "Why can there not be a hell?"

"Glad you asked. There ain't no hell because everything in the whole universe is God. God is everything that *is*—and I mean *everything*. How and why, would God make a hell out of Himself and then send Himself there? Does that make sense? Why would He need or want to punish Himself? That kind of thing is a human trait; we must not give human faults to that which is not human."

She thought for a while and mused, "It does seem strange that He would make a hell out of Himself. It is not very logical—as you would say. Okay, no hell, what about Satan?"

"Satan?? Give me a break."

She shrugged, "I guess that was a dumb question. Sorry."

He continued, "By the way, I'm calling God a *Him,* only because that is the way we have been taught to think. Actually, I also call God a Her, because She is, and also an *It* and a *Force* and anything else you wish to call or think of God to be. God has an infinity of faces by which He may be called or seen—all are valid and none are wrong."

"Wait," she said quickly, "let me think a minute. Do you mean all those statues and things they call God, like in India and in the jungles and places like that, those things are really God?"

"Sure, why not? If your church can have all kinds of statues and icons of Jesus and Mary and the zillion saints—whom no one living has ever seen—why not allow the same right to a Hindu or Buddhist? The Hindu may view his God a little differently than Christians, but he also has a trinity. His trinity is Brahma, Vishnu and Shiva—which means, God in three of Her many aspects. Brahma is God the Creator, Vishnu is the aspect of God that sustains the universe, and Shiva is God in the role of the destroyer of all things in its time. God creates, sustains and destroys—all in His cycles of being the Universe ... I think I strayed a bit off your original question about ..." he paused, trying to remember, "What *was* your question anyway?"

He could feel her smile against his neck when she answered, "I think it was about hell."

"Oh yes ..." after pausing to re-group his thoughts, he continued. "The idea of a hell was invented by priest-types to create fear in the people. Then the same priest-types came along and gave those 'shaking masses' a hope of salvation ... but only *if*—and there were a lot of *ifs*. But happily, if enough sacrifice and money was expended in the right places, those *ifs* could be glossed over.

"Now don't get me wrong; I'm not picking on your Catholic priests. I am picking on all the professions that preach hell and damnation as a means of pushing their product—and filling their pockets. I'm sure you can detect my deep down respect for the profession. Ooh sure, there may be a lot of good folk out there preaching the gospel, and doing a great job of spreading the word to those who need it in this lifetime. My own grandfather was a Baptist minister, and I hear he was great at helping the lost find their way ... But then, that isn't answering your question about hell, is it."

She shrugged, "That's okay, I know you will get there eventually."

"Okay, like I said, if God is all there is in the universe—and we shall agree to agree on that statement—then everything is God, even the space between the infinite number of pieces—that too is God. God made it all out of Himself. In the beginning was God and nothing has changed. Oh, it has been rearranged a little—change is life and life is change—but it is *all* God. If we define God as being *good,* it would mean hell is good also. So what's the purpose?"

He continued, "If God doesn't judge us—and He does not—then who is going to send us to hell? The priest? The Pope? The whole thing doesn't compute. Am I making myself clear, my love?"

She stirred in his arms and tugged at the blanket, wrapping it around the both of them, and said, "I understand most of it, but most of what I do not understand is because of my English. We must have many more talks before I understand as much as you. But ... if everyone believed there is no hell, then there would be no reason to be good and everybody would do just as they want ... Would that be good?"

"Do you think the world would exhibit any perceptible change? Is the world a better place now, because all the people who are good, are good because they fear the punishment of hell? Nooo, mi luv, unless the good we exhibit has its origin in love it is only an investment in greed and the hope of something better after death. And that is only another form of selfishness."

She squinted in thought, shrugged then said, "Okay, you have told me about hell, now how about heaven."

He shuffled, searching for the words, "Heaven is not a place; it is a state of being. We have been in that state countless times, and we shall be there countless times again. We come and we go through a million lifetimes. It is something like flying through broken clouds; we are in the sunlight one moment, then suddenly we are blind and confused as we grope through another cloud—then just as suddenly—we are once again in the brilliant sun-swept blue heaven. The clouds are the lives we grope in today—searching for the infinite light of heaven ..."

◆　　　◆　　　◆

In the story, Harry, Laurina's elderly friend dies and she mourns his passing. She is younger than John, and she worries about losing *him* in much the same way as Harry. John teases her ...

"Ha! Why do you think this old gringo wants a young and beautiful señorita? You will always be young and beautiful to me—because I will be dead long before *you* can become old."

Her face darkened; "Do not talk about death. You must not die while I am alive—never.

He stood and took her hands, "Come inside, I just remembered something I would like to read to you."

He took from a shelf his copy of Gibran's THE PROPHET and read to her about death, *"For life and death are one, even as the river and the sea are one ... "*

She touched his lips with her fingertips, her signal for him to pause, "Tell me about death, John ... so I can stop crying about Harry."

He closed the book and set it aside, took her hand and kissed it saying, "I know Harry's death has hurt you deeply, and I have wanted to say the right things to heal your hurt, but you want me to talk about something that is *not*. There is no such thing as death. We cannot die, because we were never born. The life that inhabits our body is eternal. **Never was there a time when we were not, and there never will be.** We come, we experience, we do what we have come to do in this life, and then we return *Home*. This we have done countless times before, and shall do countless times again.

"We may never know—in this lifetime—why Harry came into our lives, but whatever it was, it was for the best. His mission was finished and he went home—he returned to the One—the place he wanted to be."

"John, I know you have told me about life and death and that I do not have to fear death, and it is because of you I do not fear, but I do not want to lose you—ever. I do not know how I could go on living without you. Please, please, mi amado, do not die before me."

He pulled back and teased, "Ooh hoo, so it is all right for me to live in pain without you, but you don't want to feel that pain yourself ... Well!!"

"Do not tease me, you know what I mean."

He held her closer and kissed her forehead, "I'm sorry, I make jokes at the wrong time. Okay, I promise not to die for another one hundred years—at least; well, at least until you no longer care. Hummm, I wonder how long *that* will be?"

She threw her arms around his neck, "Never, never, never, never will I no longer care. I will love you forever, even after I die."

He kissed her ear that was pressed against his lips and said, "It seems I said, in my poem that brought us together, *forever is in the hands of Eternity, and we have but a moment* ... But then ... is not Eternity and a moment of Eternity the same? We have a love that can never be greater than at this moment, even if we live another thousand years. Now *is* forever, because if an asteroid hit this house right now, our love and we would be instantly in the hands of Eternity. So, let us live this, our moment of Eternity *now* ... and our next moment as Forever."

"Tell me about heaven, John."

"Heaven? What can I tell you about heaven that you don't already know but have merely forgotten? The truth is, I have forgotten too, and so you will just have to remember, or wait until we can explore it together—again."

"Do you think Harry went to heaven?"

"Of course, there is no other place to go. Remember my dissertation on that subject? We couldn't go to hell if we wanted to, so stop working at it, you little devil." He kissed her, and with his tickling fingers made her squirm and giggle. They played and wiggled on the couch, Scooter joined in and made them laugh all the more until they were both on the floor, couch cushions and all.

She embraced him, "I do not want to talk about death anymore. Talk to me about love and life and our happiness together—forever."

They rested in each other's arms, Laurina's soft sweatshirt had pushed up to her neck in their play, exposing her beauty to John's lips; and their thoughts of death gave way to their acts of living, and loving and knowing their moments of ecstasy—*now*."

◆   ◆   ◆

You can see, I have no qualms about mixing life, love and philosophy—and why not—does not philosophy come from life? Can philosophy be valid without a love of the Truth; and can we separate the elements of the universe into what is and is not? John believes that God is infinite, and because infinity includes all that is, has been and ever will be, and includes also that which is happening, ever has happened and ever will happen, God and the universe are a unity. He explains this to Laurina in answer to another of her questions …

"They were sitting on the couch. Laurina had her legs pulled up and she sat facing him. Her fingers toyed with the hair at the back of his head, as they watched the Discovery Channel. She turned to him during a commercial, and almost as though thinking aloud, asked,

"Do you think some people can see into the future?"

John looked up and around the room, as if looking for the source of a voice she'd heard and he hadn't, "Say what? Where'd that come from?" She made a little fist and hit him on the shoulder.

She explained, "There is a woman who lives near me; people say she can see into the future. Years ago I asked her if I would ever find true love. She told me I would, but he would not be tall and handsome like young girls dream. My true love would come from far away, and his beauty would come from his heart and his mind, and he would see my inside beauty and love me for it. She told me this, many years before I met you and it scares me, because it has come true. Do you think she could really see into the future?"

He grinned and asked, "Do you want a *during a commercial* answer, or a *Thanks for sharing with me Dad, but I didn't really want to know all of* that, Lia answer?"

She smiled, having heard his funny stories about his daughter, and said, "A Lia answer."

He reduced the TV volume and took her hand, kissed it and held it to his lips while he thought; he kissed it again and put it in his lap, holding it with both his large, gentle hands.

"Well, yes," he said, "some can see the future better than others. We've all had glimpses of the future now and then; I have, you have—though we may not have known it at the time. I remember one glimpse I had back in my college days ... I'll tell you about it some-day."

"Why not now?"

"Porque."(because) He continued, "We are *all* connected with the future and the past, because in reality, there is no future—there is no past—there is only *now*. The past is in our mind; the future is in our mind; only *now* is real. Think about that for a moment."

After a moment he continued, "Our memory of the past is in our mind, is it not? Our thinking about the future is also in our mind. What we see, do, and think right now is the only thing we can be sure of—and we can't always be sure of that; some say even *now* is an illusion."

Not wanting to lose her, he quickly explained, "Don't try to understand everything right now, I will clear up any confusion later, mi amor—maybe."

He paused for a moment to see if there were any questions forthcoming, then continued, "You see, time is a *human* concept. There is no need for time in God's universe. He doesn't need it to keep track of things. We use time as a way of saying, we are *here* at this moment, we will be *there* in another moment, and we were *over there* a moment ago. It goes with the idea of *is, was,* and *will be.*

"Do you remember I once told you, we are all a small part of God?" She nodded. "Well, as a part of God, we are a part of all that *is*. We cannot *go* anywhere—we are *already* there; we are a unity. Therefore, as a unity, we are part of *all* that is happening, *all* that has already happened, and *all* that will ever happen; and because everything is a unity—everything is happening at this *very instant*—therefore, there is no *time*."

He paused, "I want you to think about that and understand before I go on."

She smiled, "Well, I can think about it all night, but I won't promise to understand. I am afraid I will have to ask you to explain again mañana—in *Spanish.* " She giggled. "Please go on."

"Okay Luv, mañana, but to get back to your question … Some of us, who are living in what we shall call *now,* have the gift to remember better than others and they realize they can tap into their memory of what is happening this very instant—which is also the *future.* They are not seeing into the future, they are seeing *now."*

She moved closer and put her forehead on his shoulder, looked down at her hands in his, and spoke softly, "I think my head hurts, but I will think more about what you say and maybe thinking will make it clear. Tell me more, mi maestro."

He smiled and kissed her head resting on his shoulder, and brushed his cheek against her hair. She looked into his eyes and said, "It is very difficult for me to understand there is not really a past and there is no future. How can we remember what is not or has never happened?

"Actually, *everything* is about *remembering,* but I'll get into that another time."

"Why should we worry about tomorrow if there *is* no such thing?" She challenged.

"Por qué," he answered, "The words that both asks, *why* and answers *because.* I must admit, I don't have it fully clear in my own mind either, but to answer one question … you do not need to *worry* about tomorrow."

She sat quietly, thinking, and then jumping ahead. "If there is no yesterday and no tomorrow, why are we here now?"

He thought for a moment, "We are here because we *want* to be. We decided, before we were born, we wanted to experience exactly what we are experiencing right now, in this lifetime, both the good *and* the bad"

She scowled at him—questioning, "Do you mean I *wanted* to suffer the pain I had when I was eighteen? I can understand why I would choose the joy I have now—here with you—but the pain? I am not a—what is that word you taught me—masochist?"

He smiled and asked, "If you could keep the past as it is with all its bad memories, or erase all the pain you had then *but* at the price of losing all the *joy* you've had; would you pay that price—to forget the pain?"

She squinted and asked, "You mean, I could wipe out all the pain I had before, but in order to wipe that pain out of my memory, I would have to give up all the joy I have now, and also have to forget all the joy I have had with my son?" He just nodded his head.

She thought for a few moments, let out a large sigh and with conviction said, "No."

"No, what?"

"No, I would not give up my joy for *anything.*"

"And so it is;" He smiled into her eyes, "we know our joy *because* we know our despair. They are both different sides of the same coin. We cannot possibly know one without the other. A poet once said, *The self same well from which we draw our joy, we often draw our sorrow.* It cannot be any other way. It is all very simple—and beautiful—if you think about it."

She pondered what he'd said, and a tear slowly rolled down her cheek. He took her face gently in his hands and kissed the tear away, and then held her to him for a long moment until she sighed, "I do not understand all you have told me, but I think it is beautiful."

She was silent with her thoughts for a long moment before asking, "But why? Why are we here to experience all this pain and all this joy?"

"Woman, you ask the question Man has been asking since he started walking on two legs." She didn't even blink, but continued looking at him, waiting for an answer she was sure was forthcoming. He pulled her back to him, held her and caressed her forehead with his cheek and looked deep into his thoughts before he answered, **"We are here so that God can experience Himself through us."** He repeated so she would not forget, "We are here so that God can experience Herself through us."

She frowned, "I don't think I understand. Why cannot God experience for Himself?"

He thought for a moment and then continued, "Think how it would be if *you* were all you could experience. Let us imagine you are in a totally dark room, you are immersed in a tank of body-temperature water floating with your head out of water; you breath body-temperature air—your body is fed all its needs, but you do not experience food. There is nothing for you to see, or touch, or smell, or hear—you only *exist*—and you have been this way since your birth. You have no memories; you cannot even think, because you must think in terms of pictures or words; and you have never experienced *any* of these. How do you think that would be?"

He let her think as he pressed his lips to her forehead and held them there until she spoke, "I think that would be horrible, but why do you tell me this story?"

He looked into her eyes and said, "That, my darling, is all God could experience before *you* came along and taught Him to experience Himself—through *your* experiences. You have taught Him what is joy and despair, love and hate, pleasure and pain, sorrow, hot, cold. All the things you take for granted *God* could never experience, because all there is—is God. *He* was the person in the tank—except—He could and did create the universe out of Himself, and He sent parts of Himself out to explore, and to experience Himself for Himself and through Himself."

She touched his lips with her fingertips and asked, "You mean we are all here as part of some game? God was curious, so he made us his pets—so He could watch us play and suffer and die? We think life is so very important, but in reality, we are only part of an experiment. It makes me feel like I have no real meaning—my *life* has no meaning."

"Do you mean your life would have greater meaning if you were *not* a part of God? Does your life *now* have such great meaning that you cannot imagine anything better?"

She scowled, "Ummm, I don't know ... I never thought about it that way. I can always dream of a better life."

"Can you dream any *greater* meaning in life than to be a part of God—that He has sent out to *be Himself? We* are some of the countless parts of the universe—experiencing *ourselves* because we are *all* separate parts of the *ONE,* and we are experiencing this because we *want to*—for God. And we are doing this, *not* to please Him, *not* to appease Him, *not* to build up treasures in heaven. We are doing it because we love ourselves, because we *are Love. He* is the Loved, the Lover and the Loving—and, my darling, *tat twam asi,* which means, *that thou art."*

◆   ◆   ◆

In my second novel, "The Healing Road," our philosopher, John, travels north to heal some wounds. He wanders up and down the back roads of New Mexico where he finds adventure and excuses to expound his philosophy … such as the dialog he has with a woman in a Roswell Dairy Queen …

"They continued their conversation about UFO's under a model of a flying saucer hanging above them in the D.Q.

Sarah asked him, around a bite of chili-dog, "Do you believe in 'E.T's'?"

After he sipped his shake, he asked, "You mean like that cute little guy in the movie?"

"Nooooweh, I mean do you think there's life … out there?" she motioned *out there* with a sweep of her hand—milkshake and all.

"Of course … I have absolutely no doubt there are other life-forms in the universe; it's totally illogical to think otherwise. Are they more intelligent than we are? Of course—somes is, somes isn't. Are humans standing on the top rung of the evolutionary ladder of the universe? Hell no—at least, I hope to God we aren't."

She choked at his comment and tried to laugh without making a mess. He handed her a napkin and took the milkshake container out of her hand while she collected herself. "Talking with you and eating at the same time has to be done with extreme caution. Darn you." and they laughed.

"Sorry 'bout that, Luv, I didn't know I was being funny." he grinned.

"Ooh, I don't mean it was funny, just the way you said it made me laugh. I guess you hit a sympathetic string on the harp of my mind."

She reached across the table and laid her hand on his arm as she said, "I guess there's several different ways we can go with this conversation, but I'd like to hear *your* ideas about other life in the universe."

He leaned back in his chair, hot dog consumed, but still working on his shake. "How much time do you have? Do you want a synopsis, or a full version of 'John's view of the Universe?'"

It was her turn to lean back and look over her milkshake, "I have all the time you want, but considering our lack of a cozy little cottage atmosphere—and the hardness of these seats—let's take a quickie, then I'll think up dumb questions to ask later—in the quiet of our fireside."

He smiled, detecting her change in dialog, from the *street* tone when they'd first met, to the showing of an education she'd obviously been trying to subvert. He even detected in her *fireside* comment, a hidden desire for them to share something besides motel rooms. He had to agree with her on that desire; he could take motels and living out of suitcases only so long.

"Okay, but first, do you want anything else? A cone or something?"

She surveyed the serving counter and seeing no line, said, "I'll get us a couple cones. What flavor do you want?"

"Chocolate, of course." He reached into his pocket for money.

She stayed his hand, "I still have money from the drug store, sir. I'll do the honors." She strolled toward the counter swaying her tight jeans, knowing he would be watching and smiling—which he was. He cleared away the trays while she collected their cones and returned, to sit down opposite him. She leaned across the table with an expectant, 'I'm listening' look on her face.

He began, "This Cosmic Year started about sixteen billion years ago."

"Cosmic year??"

"Cosmic Year is what I call this *cycle*; a cycle that started with the Big Bang and will continue until the universe expands to a point where it stops and then it starts to return in upon itself again to the seed-state where it all began; and then shall begin it all over again, just as it has done countless times before and shall continue to do forever." He slid a napkin across the table to her and handed her a pen saying, "If you have any questions, take notes and we'll get back to them. If you need clarification on something to facilitate your understanding, interrupt me. Okay?"

"Her eyes sparkled with full attention and she was just too beautiful not to kiss, so he took her face in his cone-free hand and kissed her lips, just firm enough to let her know he meant it.

"Where was I?" He asked, "Oh yes ... The Earth was formed about five billion years ago, and the first sign of life—a green slime on a primordial swamp—began about four and a half billion years later—give or take a couple months. There's some learned debate on that figure, but it doesn't impact my thesis.

"Man's evolution, however, didn't really get a move-on until after the last ice age, about twelve thousand years ago. Now then, if this planet had been just a little smaller, it would have cooled a little faster and we could have evolved a few thousand years earlier. There are a few more variables we could throw in there to change the timing, but again, that doesn't change my thesis ... Let's say we push the start of man's rapid evolution back to fifty thousand years ago—a blink of an eye on the face of Earth's lifetime. In less than one hundred years, man has flown from the dunes at Kitty Hawk to the edge of outer space. Where do you think we'd be now if we'd started our evolution fifty thousand years earlier, instead of—whenever?"

He paused, licked the melting cone into submission, and continued. "I'm saying all of this because there are a zillion other planets out there in the universe—planets that have the right conditions for life. Oh, not life just like us, we exist on oxygen, but not *all* life forms need oxygen. We are what we are because of the conditions of *our* planet. The conditions on other planets will cause the evolution of its life forms to be what *they* are—and what they will become.

"Remember too, there have been several mass extinctions of Earth-life during the half billion years that there's been life to mass-extinct, and each time we've had to start all over again almost from scratch ... Other planets may not have had the millions of years of setbacks in evolution that we've had.

"To add to the gap, those other planets could have been formed a billion years *before* the Earth, and could have started life forms long before this planet had cooled down enough to allow us to become the green scum we were—and some of us still are ... The life forms on those planets could be millions of years ahead of us in evolution and technical know-how ... Why couldn't they know enough about space travel that would allow them to come and look us over?"

"Don't you think we are created in the image of God?" She asked.

"Of course."

"Then wouldn't all those other people in space be just like us?"

He smiled and said, "Your Bible College 'bull shit' is starting to show. Tell me, mi luv, if that asteroid hadn't struck the Earth sixty-five million years ago and wiped out all the dinosaurs—and allowed the mammals to evolve into humans—there wouldn't *be* a Man's image for God to look like, and He'd have to look like a highly-evolved dinosaur that created God in *its* own image."

She smiled broadly and said, "No wonder there's such a battle between the evolutionists and the creationists. If the Bible thumpers ever allowed people to believe in the *real* destruction of the dinosaurs, their whole belief system would crash and burn."

"Weelll, the problem with the Bible Thumpers—and a lot of others—they have absolutely no conception of an *infinite* God. They have made Him infinitesimal to fit into their own infinitesimal minds. If we say God is this or that, we are instantly saying that He is *not* the infinite number of other things that He *is*. When we say God is *not* this or that, we are limiting Him. How can we, the finite, limit the Infinite? And while we're at it—let's not limit Her to being only a Him ..."

She smiled with glee. "Oh John, I would *love* to get you back to Tennessee and have you talk to my father—the reverend, and college Prof.'s; they'd turned blue, red and then explode."

"Never happen, Luv, I don't talk about things like that to anyone who isn't interested in thinking."

◆   ◆   ◆

And on a mountain high above Albuequerque they explore the night sky ...

"The meal and its sense of well-being accompanied them as they wandered in the darkness back to the edge of a thousand foot drop, where they looked down on the lights of Albuquerque and up to the countless points of light burning holes in the black moon-less sky.

Sarah sat on a bed of pine needles and stared at the wonder above her. "I've never been so close to the stars before, they're magnificent ... and I feel so inadequate to comprehend it all." She remained silent in her wonderment for a long time before she asked, "John?"

"Sííí?"

"Do you think there are other universes? I mean, could this universe just go on and on forever, or does it stop being *our universe* somewhere and start being another one? What do *you* think?"

He was silent for a time and thought about the universe outside of their own little world. "Weelll, Luv, if you *really* want to know how I feel about things ..."

"I do, but first lay down here beside me, I hear better that way."

Her head rested in the small of his shoulder as they lie on their backs and gazed upward, and he started ... "There is really an infinite number of universes, Sarah. We are—each one of us—separate and totally different universes."

"Wait, I think you lost me."

"Sorry. Look at it this way; we see the universe with our own unique capability to perceive—based on our unique psychological and empirical make-up." He picked up a pine needle, broke it and held it in front of her to let her sniff its fragrance. "This pine needle for instance, *You* see this needle and *I* see this needle, but we can't possibly see it exactly the same. We see it with eyes and minds that have seen a million things differently; so the needle we perceive is painted with all our own personal experiences and memories. Do you understand?"

"But it's just one simple little pine needle."

"Not really, it may be the only one in my fingers, but *my* eyes see it with the memory of all the other needles and pine trees of my whole life, and their scents and size and cones and the settings under which those memories were created. But because my memories are different from yours, we both cannot possibly see this needle in exactly the same way. Therefore, your pine needle universe and everything in it is uniquely different from mine—or anyone else's."

"Let me think a minute ..." She remained in her 'cocoon of thought' for a moment, and then asked, "So then, we both perceive those stars up there differently, and therefore each star is a different universe unto itself. Heck, we don't have to wonder about parallel universes, we *all* live in parallel universes, every day of our life. Do I make sense?"

"You betcha. I couldn't have said it better."

"Gosh, and all that from a little pine needle. Think how complicated it would be to look into our own selves ... I mean, we are much more *complex* than a pine needle."

"Oh sí, and that isn't all. We already play many different rolls—in many universes. The individual plays *himself*, but for *others*, he moves in a totally different light—the unique perception of each and everyone he touches. Therefore, we are many people in one—no more real or less real than the one we see in the mirror. Think of it as being an actor, we play the part *our* way, but each and every person who sees our performance perceives a different act and actor on the stage."

She was deep in thought, so he let her probe those depths while he watched a C-130 lumber along its flight approach to Kirtland Air Force Base, and remembered another time, another life, another universe …

She giggled, "I knew there was something wrong with the system. All the effort some people put into presenting their act to the world, and not one person in that world sees the actor the way he *wants* to be seen … But, if all these people see me as something else, which one is correct? Who is the real me?"

"Who do *you* want to be?"

"Well, I certainly don't want to be the person I've been all my life. I sure don't want to be *my* self. I'm the pits."

"Sarah, my love, your *Self* has never been touched by anything you or anyone else has done to your mind or your body. The Sarah *you* know is only a tiny part of your total self."

"Are you talking about my soul? I don't believe in souls."

"Call it anything you like, but the woman I'm holding in my arms is only one of an infinite variations on the theme of Sarah. Tell me, are you the same Sarah I picked up in the desert lo those many eons ago?"

"God, I hope not. I might not be much better, but I'm sure different. I wonder why that is, and who caused the transformation?" She turned to him and buried her face in his chest …"

◆   ◆   ◆

Later in the story, John's concept of a God is introduced—a subject he'd avoided until now because of Sarah's problems with the father's church and religion. I like to call this section, "The log universe … one homogeneous hunk of everthing."

"A stroll after a delicious dinner, a shared glorious sunset and the scene was set for stretching out before the fireplace and it's crackling fire—brandy snifters in hand and Scooter curled at their feet.

Sarah sighed, "Does it get any better than this, John?"

"Not in this life, mi Luv, not in this life."

She sat up, "In *this* life? Does that mean, you believe in an after-life?"

"To answer that question I'll have to get into the subject of the *universe according to John.*"

"I remember your saying something about 'your universe' once, but that's the last I've heard of it. Now I'd like to learn how the man I love feels about life, death and whatever's next."

He leaned back, stretched and read his thoughts on the knotty-pine ceiling before saying, "Weeelll, to tell you all that will take us into the realm of *God.* Are you sure you want to go there?"

"Yes. If *you* believe in a God, then I want to hear your thoughts on the subject."

"Ookaaay. Lemme see … *After-life*, you say … Do I believe in an after-life? What you really mean is, *a life after-death* … I don't believe in death."

"You once said you were never born. Does that fit-in with your not believing in death?"

"Right-on, mi Luv. Do you remember my saying, 'Never was there a time when I was not, and there never shall be?'"

"Yes, but I didn't understand it then and don't now."

"Then you'd better get ready, 'cause here comes the part about God … or what ever you want to call Him or Her, or It—but for just the sake of discussion—let's agree that there *is* such a thing as a Supreme Being. Okay?"

She smiled a challenge, "What if I don't agree?"

"Then the discussion ends before it begins. If you want me to prove there is a God before we discuss the idea, it isn't going to happen. As an Engineer/Philosopher I think I could argue either the pro or the con on the subject, but I don't argue about religion, it's against my religion."

"What *is* your religion?"

"Who I *am* is my religion ... I don't believe in or subscribe to any of the commercialized insanities that run rampant around the world."

She smiled her agreement, "Okay Mr. Philosophizing Engineer, we'll agree to agree that there is a Godhead."

He nodded, "Good ... Now then, if there *is* a Godhead—and a Godhead by definition must be infinite—then there is *nothing* in the universe that is *not* God. Agreed?"

"Why?"

"Remember what I said once before? ... If we say that God *isn't* everything, then we must answer the obvious question, 'What *isn't* God?' When we say something is *not* God, then we—the finite—are limiting the Infinite; and who are *we* to say what God can or cannot be?"

"Hummm, I guess you're right, but I know a lot of people who *think* they have that right ... Okay, I'll accept your definition of God."

He grinned and kissed her on the tip of the nose, "Actually, we can't have my definition either, because that would be *defining* the Infinite, and that in its self is putting a boundary around infinity ... but we won't go there right now ... Okay, if God is infinite, then there is nothing that is, or has ever been or ever will be that is not God ... and it follows, everything that is happening, or has ever happened or ever *will* happen—that too is God, because all those things are a part of infinity. Do you follow me?"

"Let me digest that a little ... they didn't teach me that in Sunday school."

"Well, let me use a *for-instance* ... take the fire there in the fireplace; if all the universe is God, then that fire is also a part of God ... God is the *flame,* He is also the *burning,* He is the *log* that burns, He is the *warmth* that is felt, He is the *feeling* of that warmth, He is *we* who are warmed, He is our *joy* of our being warmed ... I could go on for-

ever—He is Forever too. He is all that is perceived or not perceived—He is also the perceiver and the perceiving ... How we
doing?"

"Go for it."

"Okay. Now, let's squeeze the whole universe—all that *is*—into a
smaller conception ... say, this piece of firewood." He picked up and
held a small log before them. "Let's say that this log is the whole universe, everything that is, was or ever will be—right here; one con-
densed homogenous hunk of all matter, energy and thought—even
time."

"Time?"

"Sure, time is as much a part of the universe as anything else. Don't
you think?"

She frowned in thought then mused, "Hummmm. Yeah-but, I
never thought of time as something solid, like the stars and all."

"How about the space between the stars ... isn't that also a part of
the universe? How solid it that?"

She grinned and sipped her brandy, "I guess you're right, I never
thought of it that way ... What about time?"

"Time? Well, time is just a concept for humans to think about the
past, present and future. In reality, there is no past or future—it's all in
the mind as memory or anticipation. The only reality is *now,* and there
are some who'll argue the reality of *now*—saying it's all an illusion."

"Humm, I was afraid of that, these months have all been a dream."
She turned in his arms and kissed him, "A wonderful, beautiful dream;
but if I'm dreaming, I'll kill the person who wakes me up."

He smiled, "I'll second that motion." He struggled to his feet and
retrieved the brandy bottle from the kitchen, refreshed both their
glasses and sat down beside her again.

She sipped her brandy and stared into the fire, thinking before she
asked, "All that's very interesting, but what about an after-life?"

"Oh yeah, I forgot what we started with … After-life, yes, well if all that *is,* is right here in this log—including birth, life, death and whatever—where do we spend an after-life?"

She was silent in thought for a long moment, "Weeell, if heaven and hell are a part of the universe, then I guess we'd have to spend it in this log too."

"And if the log is one homogeneous hunk of everything—and *everything* is God—then we too are a part of that God—the One. And everything that is, was or ever shall be is in that One also. Hence, our birth, life and death are One, all happening at this very instant … as are all the millions of lives we have ever lived and shall live … That is why I said many weeks ago, I was never born, therefore, I can never die … referring to the *self* which presently inhabits this mound of flesh you and I call *John.*"

"Ya-but, what about that flesh? *It* isn't going to be around forever."

"Oooh? Why not? Every cell in my body has been replaced many times in my lifetime. After *I* quit this 'mortal garb' all these atoms will still be around; they may be buzzing around in different molecules, but they'll still be around—somewhere—as something."

She was silent, then let out a great sigh, "Whoa, and I only wanted to know if you believe in a God."

He chuckled, "It reminds me of something Tia might say, 'Thanks, Dad, but I didn't really want to know all that.'"

"No, I *did* want to know all that, I just didn't know there was so much to think about God. I was brought up believing God was an all-powerful and vengeful guy with a flowing white beard, throwing down bolts of hellfire and damnation at all us sinners … Yeah, what about all us sinners, where do we fit into this fire log? And Satan, where is *his* log?"

"*Us* sinners? Speak for yourself, Jane."

"Oh, don't you think we're gonna to be punished for all this fornicating we've been doing?" She grinned into her brandy snifter.

John chuckled, "Your father might call it fornicating, I call it *love;* and in our 'God-log,' it can't be anything else but *pure* love, my love."

She snuggled up close to him, "You shore know the right things to say to a gal, padner."

"Did I answer your question?"

She frowned into the firelight, "What *was* my question? Oh yeah, about an after-life. Lemme think, well … you didn't really answer my question about Satan … and Hell."

"How come you haven't asked me about Heaven? Do you fear Hell more than you yearn for Heaven?"

She grinned, "Ya know, I think you hit the nail on the head; my learning about God, has been more of *fear* than of love … and the fear of Satan who's always lurking around, just waiting for me to get close to his pit so he could push me in … I never had time to think about loving Jesus, I was always too busy running from Satan."

"Well, you don't have to fear Hell. Where would it be? It can't be in our log, that's all *God.* It can't be outside our log, because our log is the whole homogeneous universe. If God is all there is, then He had to have created the universe out of Himself, which means He must have created Satan also … however, I think Satan was created by somebody else, just to scare little children … and to inspire full collection plates on Sunday mornings."

She burst out laughing. "Are you sure you've never been to my father's church?"

John stood up and rearranged the fire to receive another log. He turned and knelt before her. "Sarah, yes there is an after-life. We are living in an after-life right now, one of millions we have lived and will live in the infinite cycle of God experiencing Her self. When you remember your *true self,* you will remember also that you are—at once—infinitesimal and infinite, because you too are one with the One."

◆   ◆   ◆

John speaks his truths softly and clearly, he does not try to impress anyone with his knowledge of the English language, and thus lose the reader in a bramble of obscure words. I try to convey an open-ended idea, to inspire the reader to *think*. The problem I have found, however, there are too few readers who want to think—it must be the TV mentality.

I have often wondered, "Does the young person who wanders through life with music-blasting headphones stuck in his ears do so to drown out any stray intelligent thought that may escape from his brain and into his consciousness?" Would he know what to do with an intelligent thought should it light that blown-out flame within *his* brain? Could he cope with such a flickering candle in the darkness of our modern world? Is he the *Man With a Hoe—Twenty-first Century*? We might ask, as does Edwin Markham's poem, "... Whose breath blew out the light within this brain? ..." Was it television sit-coms, Rap 'music,' no-brain movies or a plethora of other forms of entertainment that have comparable brain-numbing effects? Those winds may blow in different ways through different brains, but the result is the same.

If my reader has traveled thus far in this book, I would like to assume the winds of our world of *materials* have not blown out the light within your brain, and you might give thought to the ideas I have tried to share with you.

8

IN SUMMATION

Many Christmas vacations have come and gone since Mr. Krause read the words of my short story to that English Class in January of 1947; now I sit before a computer screen and search for words to express the meaning of it all—if there *is* a meaning to it all ...

Who is to answer the question that has been asked by mumbling lips on faces that look upward and ask, "Why?? I now return to those days of innocence, when life stretched out ahead of me beyond the horizons of my imagination ...

WHY?

It was a warm summer evening in northwestern Michigan. The war in Europe was over and the Japs were being pushed back across the Pacific island by island. This was in the days before light pollution, so the stars were incredibly bright and incomprehensibly numerous to Joe and me as we lie on a Lake Michigan sand dune. We two sixteen year old boys would usually spend a night like this talking about girls or about going off to war, but tonight ... tonight the darkness and the stars compelled us to silence. Only the distant gentle lapping of the waves on the beach and an occasional night bird gave witness to our Earth-bound reality—and that we were not actually drifting in space.

This was before the concept of the 'Big Bang;' before men spoke about distances in terms of millions of light years. It was before we knew the universe was sixteen billion years old and contained millions of galaxies. It was when we could actually *see* the Milky Way—that great white path across the blackness—and we two didn't even know it was 'our' galaxy. It was all wonderful and mysterious and beyond the compass of our young brains.

We lie there for what seemed hours, before questions came to us to ask about this totality that absorbed us ... How many stars were there? Were there other beings somewhere up there? Could there be more stars beyond those we could see with our eyes, and maybe even other universes. How far could the sky go—even forever? And what was there *before* the stars? We were taught in Sunday School that God had made the heavens and Earth, but ... somehow that story just didn't seem grand enough to serve this *incredible* evening.

Long we lie there and thought and talked and thought some more, until our heads seemed to hurt. The final summation of it all—that broke the spell and our flight through time and space—was when I asked of that awesome blackness ... WHY??

A lifetime of summers have come and gone since that night on the dune, along with half a century of colleges and philosophies and sermons by learned men. Many years have I seen the advance of sciences that allow us to see deep into that universe—and deep into ourselves. Science has taught me to understand the drift of the continents and the creation of our universe. I have learned about black holes in the heavens, and read about black souls on Earth. I have heard men speak of heavens and hells, of Gods and devils. I have heard that my soul is damned to eternal fire if I don't follow just the *right* path—but I have heard that my soul is forever perfect and untouched by my efforts past, present or future. I have heard the finite try to define the Infinite, and I have heard the finite deny the Infinite. I have heard that someday there will be a light in the heavens, and God will return to reclaim His faithful; and I have heard that someday the universe will cease its headlong flight to infinity ... and return again to the seed from which it sprang—and start the whole process over again. All these things, and more, have I heard and learned—and yet ... after all this, the question remains ... WHY?

Why, if in fact there is a God did he create the universe and then why did He create Man? Was He lonesome? Was He curious to see how it would all turn out—and so He is conducting one great experiment? Did Man just happen? Did God create Man or did Man create God? ... In a few million years—after Man has destroyed himself and the insects have evolved into the 'highest life-form'—will the insects create a new God in *their* own image? If the Earth or the universe did not exist, would God still exist? Does God have to be conceived by Man to exist?

The answers to these questions from the great learned men of the cloth might be, *We mustn't trouble ourselves about those weighty questions ... There are some things in life that we cannot be expected to understand ... When God wants us to know, he will let us understand ...* These *excuses* I can accept without argument; it is to those who propose to know *all* the answers I give argument."

◆   ◆   ◆

In my philosophies I have proposed to know the answers. The small candle that flickers in my brain gives light to those words whispered to me in the silence of my 'closet;' all may not be *my* words, and even though they have found their way through my fingers and onto these pages, they are not meant to convince, but only to share with the reader. If even one line has caused you to think, to wonder or even to ponder, then my efforts have not been in vain; you have been ready, and I welcome you to the *Lonely Road*

EPILOGUE

It is now 2007 and the world is in chaos—much the same as it has always been, but it is now on a global scale—devoid of reason at any level—a world ruled by a greed of power that defies resolution.

I have often been heard to say, "I have a solution to the whole problems of this world faces—another six mile wide asteroid." Yes, another asteroid like the one that wiped out the dinosaurs would take care of Man's problems—but to be consistent with the philosophy in my novels—it would not make one jot or tittle difference in the whole scheme of things. I cannot help but wonder if there isn't another way …

In the grand experiment of His universe, is He receptive to exploring new solutions to old problems? How would we know? Whom do we ask? The priests? The Bible thumping whatsits? The sword-wielding mullahs? The learned PhD's of 'infinite wisdom?' Whom do we ask to show us a way back to the Garden of Eden … or to where ever that pretty story was meant to depict?

In my novels, John has found a few answers in his Voice. "Voice" is a name I gave to the source of John's help in his life of confusion and frustration. That source's voice found its way though my fingertips and onto my computer, and I often wondered who spoke the words I never heard but often wrote. Now I wonder … if I asked the *big* question—the survival of the human race—would that source whisper the answer to my ear of ears. I wonder and I ask … and I listen … But … if I ask and I listen and I hear and I write … will those who read the words understand what I have written?

Let the *Voice* now speak through my fingertips …

I have spoken words to millions before you, I have written words on tablets of clay, on walls of stone, on leaves of paper through pens of feathers and pencils of carbon. These words have I put on paper with typewriters and computers to feed the thousands of presses that make millions of books, but the reading of words can change the lives of only a few. The Buddha heard my words and taught that, only in the freedom from ignorance can Man escape the misery of life; but from the sowing of ignorance, Man still reaps the grief of his greed. The ignorance of power causes men to trample on the backs of the lowly—to build temples and pyramids toward a coveted paradise in the sky; they know not in which direction I reside. They curse the Satan below, but know not the house wherein he dwells. They slay their brothers in my name, but know not a single breath of my being. Poets write words of the futility of life—this 'brief light twix dark and dark'—but to those who hear and understand my words there is no darkness—not in the deepest black sky above or deepest hole below—there is no darkness. To him who would find the light, he will not find it in the written word, nor will he find it in the shouted words that spiel forth from the mouths of greed—those who steal gold from begging cups of the blind.

I have spoken my guidance to the ears of those before you, and though they sought to make men understand, the ears of Man heard naught but the ringing of their greed for power and the call of earthly rewards …

And what of you? Will you listen to the words I whisper to your ear of ears? Will you see with your eye of eyes? Will you comprehend the light I show you? And if you do all these things, will you cast your crumbs upon the waters in hope that it will return a loaf? Will you shout your truth from the pulpit to the deaf and blind, or will you cry in despair of their ignorance.

No, you have ears to hear, therefore I will tell you what you already know but have merely buried beneath the burden and distractions of this life. And when you have remembered, listen for the silent screams of those who stumble in their own darkness; tell them to listen and I will whisper to their ear of ears.

The words I speak to them will not solve the problems of the world—even if they shout it from the mountaintop—not one other will hear and understand what I have spoken. Each man must hear the truth that dwells within his own True Self and let it guide his own way. Neither can he guide the way of others, for each man has his own truth and his own path to be trod alone ... And, indeed, it can be a very lonely road, for few there will be whom you meet along its rocky way and none with whom you can truly share its golden light.

978-0-595-45383-2
0-595-45383-X